THEATRE SYMPOSIUM

A PUBLICATION OF THE SOUTHEASTERN THEATRE CONFERENCE

Theatre and Space

Volume 24

Published by the

Southeastern Theatre Conference and

The University of Alabama Press

THEATRE SYMPOSIUM is published annually by the Southeastern Theatre Conference, Inc. (SETC), and by the University of Alabama Press. SETC nonstudent members receive the journal as a part of their membership under rules determined by SETC. For information on membership, write to SETC, 1175 Revolution Mill Drive, Studio 14, Greensboro, NC 27405. All other inquiries regarding subscriptions, circulation, purchase of individual copies, and requests to reprint materials should be addressed to The University of Alabama Press, Box 870380, Tuscaloosa, AL 35487–0380.

THEATRE SYMPOSIUM publishes works of scholarship resulting from a single-topic meeting held on a southeastern university campus each spring. A call for papers to be presented at that meeting is widely publicized each autumn for the following spring. Information about the next symposium is available from the incoming editor, Becky K. Becker, Center for International Education, Columbus State University, 4225 University Avenue, Columbus, GA 31907, becker_becky@columbusstate.edu.

THEATRE SYMPOSIUM
A PUBLICATION OF THE SOUTHEASTERN THEATRE CONFERENCE

Volume 24   *Contents*   2016

Introduction

Becky K. Becker

"We are now at least equally likely to look at the theatre experience in a more global way, as a sociocultural event whose meanings and interpretations are not to be sought exclusively in the text being performed but in the experience of the audience assembled to share in the creation of the total event."
—Marvin Carlson, *Places of Performance*

Theatre and Space is a wide-ranging topic, opening discussion to myriad spatial arrangements, architectural styles, and historical contexts. Yet despite the global nature of the theme, no discussion of theatre and space quite works without consideration of the audience as central to the spatial relationships created. Whether we are reflecting upon the ancient Greek theatre with its semi-circular audience arrangement wrapping around the playing space, or the contemporary trend of immersive spaces in which audience members are often free to move about at will, our use of space in the theatre is intentional and inextricably linked to how we hope the audience will be impacted. We utilize space in particular ways to engage audiences in the storytelling experience; without the presence of a live audience, our efforts though not meaningless lack immediacy, as evidenced by recent "live" television broadcasts of popular musical theatre offerings such as *Peter Pan* and *The Wiz*. To that end, how effectively do different theatre spaces function? Is there a particular spatial relationship that lends greater impact to imagery in the theatre and, thereby, meaning? How have theatrical spaces changed over time? What happens when non-theatre spaces are used for theatrical performance? Is there a "politics" of space? Can space be "gendered"? And what happens when the performance space is a virtual space, rather than a physical one? These and many other questions were considered as thirty-five theatre scholars/practitioners gathered for Theatre Symposium 24, April 10–12, 2015, on the campus of Agnes Scott College in Decatur, Georgia. Regardless of our focus on theatre and space, nearly every conversation that we had during our time together inevitably led us back to a living, breathing aspect linking them together: the audience.

In a time when so many options for entertainment are easy to access, it is no surprise that theatre practitioners and scholars are preoccupied with the role of the audience. While space undoubtedly impacts the rehearsal and production processes, its greater significance seems to rest in the impact a specific location and its use has on the audience. As Marvin Carlson observed in his keynote presentation, the theatre lobby functions as a kind of "mimetic airlock," ushering audiences into theatrical space, presumably preparing them for their encounters with mimetic expression. Likewise in his closing remarks, Carlson aptly pointed to the ways in which audience expectations are sometimes thwarted—and possibly ignited—by nontraditional uses of space and nonmimetic performance modes. Whether traversing traditional theatre spaces—as discussed by symposium presenters Gregory Carr in his research on the African Grove Theatre; Tony Gunn in his examination of Edward Gorey's theatrical designs; and George Pate in his reflection on Beckett's stage directions—or venturing through decidedly innovative spaces—as described by J. K. Curry in her examination of Theatre for One; Susan Kattwinkel in her reflection on cultural spaces; Carla Lahey in her discussion of modern uses of medieval sacred spaces; Elizabeth Kling in her description of classical opera recontextualized in a bar setting; and Christopher Peck in his analysis of the immersive production *Then She Fell*—the audience's essential role is to complete the theatre-and-space relationship. For without the audience there is no one to observe the traditional "fourth wall" of realism, witness the transgressing of that wall, or mingle with actors and other viewers in an immersive setting. Without an audience, the performance space becomes a kind of void, lacking the necessary component to let it live. Or does it? According to symposium presenter (and author in this volume) Lisa Marie Bowling, theatre spaces hold their own materiality, evoking "life" experiences that mark and shape their existence. Yet even in light of philosophical conceptions of a building's richly storied materiality, space is indelibly empowered by the audience's presence, filling the void with perceivers who in turn proliferate meanings. Paralleling the critical importance of the audience, a discussion of power emerged during Theatre Symposium 24 encompassing both generative depictions of power, as in Haley Flanders' and Katrina Dunn's papers on Blue Man Group and Canada's National Arts Centre, respectively, and more destructive iterations of power, as discussed by James Hardy in his ruminations on surveillance and Laine Newman in her analysis of identity and space. Whether positive or negative in scope, meanings generated within theatre spaces are impacted by the cultural contexts from which they emerge, wielding power over the ways in which space is conceived, scrutinized, and experienced. As a result, the relationship between space and theatre *and* audience is diverse, complex, and ever changing in practice.

In ways similar to the symposium weekend, this volume provides diverse viewpoints on theatre and space, as well as its relationship to the audience. Sebastian Trainor and Samuel T. Shanks offer contemporary perspectives on two ancient theatre spaces, while Lisa Marie Bowler describes the Globe Theatre, a replica of the original, as embodying a kind of absence despite its rich link to the past. Focusing on distinctly different periods and settings, both Andrew Gibb and Christine Woodworth describe a politics of space in which specific players gain prestige and power. Chase Bringardner identifies the audience as playing an important role in creating a space for parody in a historic Nashville venue, while Arnab Banerji describes an exhausting process for members of the Bengali group theatre who must continually move from space to space. Finally, Alicia Corts discusses virtual performance spaces and the degree to which participants are able to control their online identities within virtual performances. Bookending these eight essays are Marvin Carlson's keynote presentation "Whose Space Is It Anyway?" and his closing remarks for the symposium, both of which allude to, and richly explicate, the ultimate arbiters of theatrical space: the audience.

Like the relationship to the audience, which is so intertwined in discussions of theatre and space, a symposium (and, for that matter, a journal) is a collaborative effort. Having penned upwards of twenty books, Marvin Carlson, keynote presenter and respondent for this year's Symposium, generously offered his expertise on theatre and performance spaces. In addition to a kind, inclusive manner, Carlson's near-marathon dedication to seeing live theatre over the span of more than five decades infused the symposium with collegial familiarity and herculean insight. Likewise, David S. Thompson, the Annie Louise Harrison Waterman Professor of Theatre at Agnes Scott College, our past editor and Symposium 24 host, not only provided invaluable guidance as preparations were made for the occasion, but also did the groundwork that allowed symposium participants to fully enjoy the spectacular venue on his home campus. As is invariably the case with Theatre Symposium, the presenters and participants shape the rich conversation that emerges. This year was no exception, which allowed participants to revel in a scholarly experience that is both challenging and invigorating—a quality that has kept me coming back nearly every year since my first Symposium in 2008. Given my appreciation for Theatre Symposium as an influential scholarly outlet over the years, I am especially grateful to J. K. Curry, Philip G. Hill, Scott Phillips, David S. Thompson, and Bert Wallace for their patience and guidance.

They may not know this, so it seems appropriate to mention it here, but when I was asked to serve as editor for Theatre Symposium volumes 24 and 25, it meant a great deal to me because I have come to respect and admire each of them for their dedication to theatre scholarship and generative discourse—and for providing a scholarly home to all variety of theatre educators and practitioners in the Southeast and beyond. This volume would not have been possible without the careful work of the Theatre Symposium editorial board in reviewing submissions and providing insightful commentary. I cannot thank them enough for their work in this capacity. Thanks also to Betsey Horth and the staff at the SETC central office, as well Daniel Waterman and the editorial staff of the University of Alabama Press, who have generously answered questions and provided much-needed support—often with humor and always with kindness. Associate editor Sarah McCarroll deserves high praise for her thoughtful work on this volume; how fortunate am I to have a collaborator who is, in short, simpatico. Finally, to my husband, Mark Jarzewiak: thank you for supporting the many twists and turns my academic adventure has taken; most of all, thank you for being my favorite member of the audience.

Keynote Address

Whose Space Is It, Anyway?

Marvin Carlson

The normal image of a theatrical performance is one that takes place inside a space particularly created for such activity. Almost all theatrical cultures have developed some sort of performance space set apart from the normal world of human activity, a space that serves as a site of imagination subject to certain rules, a fundamental one being that the audience agrees to serve as spectators and accept the fictive world the actors present to them. The performance space itself thus serves as a kind of "frame" emphasizing this dynamic (indeed, an alternative name for the proscenium arch theatre is the "picture-frame stage," and some late nineteenth-century British theatres in fact surrounded the stage on all four sides with an ornate frame). In most cases this performance space, the stage and auditorium, is not even entered directly from the outside world, but is separated from that world by a liminal area, as a kind of mimetic airlock, the theatre lobby, which allows audiences to move by stages into the illusory realm of the theatre.

Theatrical performances that were not "protected" by this house of illusion have been much more susceptible to incursions from the physical world. Even the classic Greek stage, forming a partial enclosure, could and apparently did take advantage of the "real world" accessible to its audiences, the open sky above them. Thus, many of the extant plays, among them *Oedipus* and *Antigone*, begin at or near dawn, and it is difficult to imagine that the plays which were presented at that time of day did not take advantage of this contribution from the real world.

In the very earliest liturgical dramas of the Middle Ages we find already a complex mixture of theatrical elements and real spaces. Early liturgical drama was staged in parts of medieval cathedrals, but although these were real locations, they were accepted as suitable symbolically, reinforcing the effect of the performance on an emblematic if not on a realistic level. When religious dramas began to be performed outside the cathedrals, the utilization of the physical surroundings became much more complex. Often these plays remained in the vicinity of the cathedral, particularly on its wide front platform and steps, and the cathedral performed not merely as a rich decorative background, like the classic Roman scenic façade, but also in its "true" role as the abode of God and the angelic choirs.

In some cases this "theatricalization" of real places could involve a large part of the city, most notably in the Passion processionals that are still echoed in the widespread Via Dolorosa process of modern times. As early as the fifteenth century, the city of Vienna staged the public humiliation of Christ in the city marketplace, and then the actor bore his cross through the winding streets of the city to the distant cemetery where the crucifixion and resurrection were to be enacted. The market, the streets, the cemetery, and even the watching public were thus elements of the real world imaginatively refigured as parts of the universal city, Jerusalem.[1] There is still of course a certain slippage between the Vienna cemetery and what it represents, because although it is a real cemetery, it is not the site it imaginatively represents. This distinction is of particular importance in reference to sacred sites, which inevitably take on some aura of the actions that reportedly occurred there.

In fact the most ancient records that we have of theatrical activity are ritual observances carried out in specific sacred locations, which are essential to the event. The ancient Egyptian text from Abydos, whose "passion play" of Osiris is often cited as the earliest known theatrical text, was performed annually for some two thousand years, beginning in the second millennia BCE. These were presented at the most sacred site in Egypt, the island where Osiris was reportedly buried.[2] Jerusalem also witnessed theatrical activities at its major sites from very early times, as may be seen in the first detailed reports that we have from a pilgrim to that city, Egeria, in 381–84 CE. She reports a number of commemorative activities at various sacred sites, including a reenactment of the triumphal entry of Palm Sunday with "the bishop led in the same manner as the Lord once was led," accompanied by children singing hosannas and waving palm and olive branches.[3]

With the Renaissance and the movement of theatre indoors, the concept of the actor performing in any sort of "real" surrounding was almost completely lost. Even when the great baroque festivals moved outdoors, as in Louis XIV's famous *Pleasures of the Enchanted Island*, performances either occurred within a courtyard whose classic architectural background was as neutral as a Roman stage façade or in the royal park, where natural elements like trees and water had been subjected to such ruthless control that every possible trace of the natural had been removed.

A remarkable example of an almost opposite aesthetic—and one much closer to modern experimentation—was undertaken by Goethe in 1782, early in his Weimar years. Goethe invited members of the Weimar court to an evening entertainment he had devised himself, a small comic opera called *The Fishermen*. They assembled at a small pavilion in the court park appropriately called "the Cottage of the Muses." Entering the small building, they found seats arranged facing the back wall of the cottage, which had been removed to provide a frame for the actual landscape outside, a wooded glade and the bend of a stream. The audience was reportedly entranced by the sight of a real boat coming down the real stream with a singing oarsman and by the mysterious effect of lanterns carried by actors bobbing amidst the trees.[4]

It would not be an exaggeration to say that this modest court entertainment represented the most fully realized theatrical representation to date of what would come to be recognized as the Romantic aesthetic—the emphasis upon nature and the natural, upon rustic simplicity, upon the sort of atmosphere created by lanterns and moonlight. A similar impulse lay behind the interest in atmospheric scene design begun the following year in London by Garrick's designer Philip James de Loutherbourg. Both projects shared the same desire to make contact with the "real," and both sought this in the somewhat mysterious realm of nature so beloved by the Romantic imagination. The following century's theatre designers would almost without exception follow de Loutherbourg in trying to bring this reality into the theatre, but in the twentieth century Goethe's example would also become more and more followed, as the theatre began to colonize extra-theatrical space.

No one articulated more clearly than Victor Hugo the bond between nature and the real and the centrality of the real to Romantic art in general and the theatre in particular. In his best-known statement on this subject, the 1827 *Preface to Cromwell*, he asserts that "the poetry of our time" is the drama, and "the characteristic of the drama is the real." He continues: "In the drama, as it may be conceived at least, if not executed, all the parts cohere and everything happens as in real life."[5] Even though one may protest, with justification, that this hardly applies to the larger-than-life heroes and melodramatic turns of a Hugo drama, it marks out a direction that the future Realistic drama, in many ways an outgrowth of Romanticism, would follow. In the present context, Hugo's remarks on reality and scenic design are particularly important: "We are beginning to realize in our day," he observes, "that exactness in the matter of locality is one of the most essential elements of reality. The speaking or acting characters are not the only ones who leave a faithful impression upon the mind of the spectator. The place where this or that catastrophe occurred becomes an incorruptible and convincing witness to it; and the absence of this sort of silent character makes the grandest scenes of history incomplete upon the stage. What poet would dare murder Rizzio elsewhere than in Mary Stuart's chamber? To stab Henri IV elsewhere than in the Rue de la Ferronerie, blocked up with drays and carriages? To burn Jeanne d'Arc elsewhere than in the Old Marketplace?"[6] For a modern reader, this may well seem a call for the development of what would later come to be called site-specific theatre, and indeed it may be considered as helping to prepare the way intellectually for such work, but for Hugo and his contemporaries the implications of this passage were not that radical, though radical enough. He was calling for theatre settings to reflect iconically their presumed locations, differing from play to play and even, perhaps, from scene to scene, rather than relying upon the single neutral antechambers used for Racine and the tradition he represented.

For most of the following century the Romantics and the Realists who followed them worked in this direction, creating scenic designs that reflected with greater and greater realistic accuracy the locations indicated in the dramatic text. The major English director Charles Kean was honored for both the splendor of his Shakespearean productions and for the historical accuracy of their scenery. The culmination of this monumental approach to visual realism in Shakespeare came in the productions of English directors Henry Irving and Herbert Beerbohm-Tree, who, in a famous 1911 revival of *A Midsummer Night's Dream*, offered his audience live rabbits and a mossy stage floor sprouting live flowers that could be plucked by the actors. In the Realistic theatre the modern box set appeared, re-creating onstage what seemed to be a real domestic space, with real doors and doorknobs, real molding, and dimensional furniture. Like monumental realistic Shakespeare, such domestic illusions of everyday life reached their apotheosis at the turn of the next century, in this case in the work of David Belasco, perhaps the most famous champion of Realism in scenic environments. For *The Governor's Lady* in 1912, he re-created the interior of a popular chain of New York restaurants, Child's, in which the audience could even smell the coffee and pancakes being prepared. According to *Theatre Magazine*, "It is as if he had taken the audience between the intermission, walked them around the corner of Seventh Avenue and seated them to one side of the Child's restaurant at that location and let the last act be played there."[7] Of course, an important part of subsequent experimental theatre, such as promenade productions and immersive theatre, would do precisely that, converting real space into theatrical space.

An early example of such activity was undertaken by an amateur society in England, the Pastoral Players, which caused a stir in artistic circles in the mid-1880s with their outdoor productions of pastoral plays by Shake-speare and Fletcher in the Coombe Wood in South London. One review of that production observed that both actors and audience were no longer looking at canvas and "carpentry, but at realities, real rounded trees, living grass, glades and prospect. There is no sham. The sun is really shining, the birds are singing, the leaves and blades of grass and flowers really waving in the breeze."[8] In the opening years of the twentieth century, some of the greatest directors moved out of conventional theatres to utilize such non-theatrical space. Two productions, both staged in 1920, were par-ticularly outstanding examples of this. First was one of the most famous stagings by the great Max Reinhardt, his *Everyman*, which inaugurated the Salzburg Festival that year. Here, taking inspiration from the open-air productions of the medieval period, Reinhardt placed the action on a large platform set before the doors of the Salzburg Cathedral, and the entire area was incorporated into the performance, with characters enter-ing from side streets and bells rung or cries shouted at appropriate mo-ments from towers elsewhere in the city. Even nature was theatricalized, as Hofmannsthal reports: "One of these criers had been placed in the highest tower of a medieval castle, built far above the city, and his voice sounded, weird and ghostly, about five seconds after the others, just as the first rays of the rising moon fell cold and strange from the high heav-ens on the hearts of the audience."[9] The Salzburg Festival inspired some of Reinhardt's most ambitious open-air productions. In 1933 Reinhardt's designer Clemens Holzmeister built an entire small medieval village with trees, bushes, and flowers that grew from summer to summer as the pro-duction was revived. Once again, nature was pressed into theatrical ser-vice: "Moon and stars joined in the play, and gusts of the night wind led from a sultry evening to the pallid dawn of the dungeon scene."[10] The following year, Reinhardt produced one of his most striking and influen-tial outdoor productions, a production of *The Merchant of Venice* actu-ally staged in a small square in Venice in front of a palazzo that Reinhardt claimed had been the resident of a Jewish merchant in Shakespearean times and with a bridge at the rear over a small canal, along which gon-dolas passed to and fro and upon which the elegant Spanish barque of the Prince of Aragon arrived with its noble suitor.[11]

Reinhardt's productions in found locations of this type inspired a number of directors elsewhere in Europe. In Italy several Goldoni plays were presented in appropriate town squares, and in 1937 the Danish Tour-ist Board invited the British Old Vic company to present a festival produc-tion of *Hamlet* at Elsinore Castle, its presumed actual location (although the current castle was built in the sixteenth century, contemporary with Shakespeare, but centuries after the historical Hamlet, if he indeed really existed). Thus in June 1937, the Old Vic Company, headed by Laurence Olivier and Vivien Leigh and directed by Tyrone Guthrie, went to perform *Hamlet* "in his own home" or "in its rightful setting," as the British press announced it.[12] In such productions as the Elsinore *Hamlet* or the Venetian *Merchant of Venice* we seem, at least at first glance, to have literal fulfillments of Victor Hugo's vision of a performance in its correct historical location, where the walls themselves "bore silent witness" to the events. Indeed, almost this thought exactly was expressed by the Special Correspondent of the London *Times* of June 4, 1937: "The ghost not only of Hamlet's father but of all the vast and shadowy legend of the Danish Prince haunts the green roofs, the fantastic pinnacles, the dungeons, the great embattled strength of Elsinore."[13] The problem with this vision, of course, is not only that Hamlet (if he ever existed) never saw any of this architecture, or vice versa, but more importantly that the "real world" evoked here is not, as in Hugo, drawn from historical events, but from a dramatic fiction, as was the Reinhardt *Merchant*, however authentic its Renaissance palazzos and gondolas.

Just a few months after Reinhardt's *Everyman*, Nikolai Evreinov in Russia created an even more ambitious outdoor spectacle, a re-creation of the historical storming of the winter palace in St. Petersburg upon the actual location of that event, involving over 8,000 participants, tanks, armored vehicles, and even the battleship *Aurora*. Evreinov essentially echoed Hugo by stressing the fact that this work was "performed in the *actual place* where the historic event occurred."[14] Many such reenactments were presented as part of the Russian Revolutionary theatre, but the major modern vogue for battle reenactments, staged on their actual locations, enjoyed a major revival in the United States in the 1960s for the centennial of the Civil War and again in the 1970s for the bicentennial of the American Revolution. Countless battles and other historical events were re-created in their original locations with participants in authentic costume attempting to follow with varying exactness the events of a century or two before. This activity, part hobby, part recreation, has spread over the United States, then to Britain, and today is found around the world.[15]

Despite their considerable social and cultural importance, historical reenactments (with a few exceptions) have not attracted a great deal of attention from theatre historians. Nevertheless, this sort of blending of fiction, history, and real locations in fact has very close ties to a movement that has been generally acknowledged as an important part of late twentieth-century theatre: site-specific performance, created not by hobbyists or amateurs, but by professional theatre organizations as specific contributions to that art. Site-specific theatre, like much experimental theatre of the twentieth century, had its origins not in the theatre world but in the world of art. In reaction to the exclusivity and commodification of "museum" art, a number of artists in the late 1960s and early 1970s began to create works of art for specific public locations, outside the world of museum culture. By the later 1970s such work was widely recognized as a new approach and generally designated as "site-specific."

This term brought with it from the art world the idea of a work of art created for and, theoretically, fully understandable only within a particular location; but even more important than this formal concern was a political and social one. The very act of moving outside the conventional theatre, the concert hall, or the gallery was generally seen as representing a break not only with the practices of the past, but also with their exclusivity and isolation from a more general public. Site-specific theatre in its early years in particular sought out physical locations that had specific relevance to a working-class audience. Of course this orientation was closely in harmony with the increasing politicization of the experimental theatre of Europe and the United States in the late 1960s and early 1970s, but it was also surely reinforced by a major shift that was taking place in the study of history itself. As the traditional "great man" view of history began to be seriously challenged by the idea of "history from below," much early site-specific theatre turned away from figures such as Abraham Lincoln or William Tell and from re-creations of famous battles to build works based on everyday locations and everyday life.

No one expressed this aesthetic better than Armand Gatti, one of the leading experimental dramatists in France at this period, and also one of the most politically engaged. In 1964 he presented a play based on a freedom fighter in the Spanish Civil War whose story, said Gatti, could not be told in a theatre, but only in a space congenial to its subject, a factory, or a prison. The show was in fact presented in an abandoned Belgian factory, and Gatti's comments on this space provide a striking example of Hugo's image applied not to settings of the great events of history, but to the life and work of the lower classes:

> We had to make the discovery that with this kind of subject it's mostly the *place*, the architecture, that does the writing. The theatre was located not in some kind of Utopian place, but in a historic place, a place with a history. There was grease, there were acid marks, because it was a chemical factory; you could still see traces of work; there were still work-clothes around; there were still lunch-pails in the corner, etc. In other words, all these left-over traces of work had their own language. These rooms that had known the labour of human beings day after day had their own language, and you either used that language or you didn't say anything. . . . That's why I wrote in an article, "a play authored by a factory."[16]

As the term "site-specific" grew in popularity in the late twentieth century, so did its range of usage until it came to mean almost any kind of theatrical performance taking place outside a conventional theatre building.[17] Some producers, such as the British artistic team of Ewan Forster and Christopher Heighes, did not, like Gatti, place a narrative within a location, but instead sought to reveal the "language" of certain historically socially and architecturally significant buildings and locations. Still others, more like the original site-specific creators in the art world, sought to let locations inspire new original works. For the most part, site-specific theatre has dealt with urban or at least with human-created sites, but with the rise of a few interested in environmental concerns, some site-specific work turned from constructed environments to natural ones. Sunrises, moonlit night skies, bodies of water, forests, even breezes have always been a part of exterior site-specific work, but it was not until after the environmental movement of the 1970s that artists began to produce major site-specific works that, although they might involve human actors, were primarily concerned with their audience's experience of the real natural world.

The most ambitious such artist was the Canadian R. Murray Schafer, who from 1980 onward created a series of monumental works, primarily in natural locations, which together have made up his ongoing *Patria* project. *Princess of the Stars*, the third play in the cycle, begins in darkness and features the forest and lake as dawn slowly comes, the major sounds provided by awakening birds. *The Spirit Garden (Patria 10)*, first presented in 2005, involves planting seeds in its first section and the harvesting of their products in the second, for which the audience must return six months later. Real products are grown in real time and the spectators, if they choose, can also share in consuming them.

While *Patria* remains the most ambitious theatricalization of nature yet attempted, audiences have come to accept during the past half-century the ability of theatre to claim almost any real location, as it can almost any activity, as part of its domain. Although Schafer is an important exception, the great majority of the new spaces claimed by theatre in recent years have been urban spaces, where it is easier for audiences to gather. Although early site-specific works usually were planned for a conventionally passive audience, in the twenty-first century audiences are more commonly encouraged to move about in the theatricalized space, becoming to a greater or lesser extent performers themselves within that space.

This encouragement to physical involvement began with British promenade productions of the late twentieth century, a variation of site-specific theatre in which audiences were required to move to a series of different sites as the production progressed. Most commonly they were guided as a group from location to location, but in some cases, such as Reza Abdoh's major work *Father Was a Peculiar Man,* set in a several square block area of New York in 1990, or Deborah Warner's 2003 *The Angel Project,* covering a much larger part of the city, spectators had considerable freedom as to how they would visit and experience the various prepared locations.

In the twenty-first century, experimental productions that have utilized spaces outside of traditional theatres have come to be more commonly called "immersive" than "site-specific," reflecting a change from an emphasis upon the character of the space itself to an emphasis upon the audience experience within that space. The term "immersive" was popularized by the British company Punchdrunk, which has abandoned traditional theatre space to create elaborate indoor environments in multi-floored abandoned structures of all sorts, allowing audiences to wander according to their own choice within these spaces. Their *Macbeth*-flavored production *Sleep No More* was brought to New York in 2003 and became one of the most popular successes of the new century, still running today, more than a decade later.[18] Its success has inspired countless other so-called "immersive" productions, such as *Speakeasy Dollhouse,* set in several adjoining locations presumably in the 1920s, which encourages audience members to come in costume and interact (in character) with the inhabitants of these created spaces. Even more elaborate immersive productions have been mounted in Europe by groups like Rimini Protokoll in Germany and Signa in Denmark. For their 2008 production of the *Ruby Town Oracle,* Signa created a complete village of twenty-two buildings, which audiences could visit at any time and for any length during its week of performance, using the spaces as if they were an actual community and interacting however they wished with the more than forty inhabitants.

Bert O. States, in his short but enormously influential book *Great Reckonings in Little Rooms,* calls attention to a particular quality of theatre as a practice. In States' words, "Theater is the medium, par excellence, that consumes the real in its realest forms: man, his language, his rooms and cities, his weapons and tools, his other arts, animals fire and water—even, finally, theater itself. Its permanent spectacle is the parade of objects and process *in transit* from environment to imagery."[19] An important part of the real that States does not specifically mention in this catalogue is the real of the space in which we exist, and in recent times, having consumed the other realities States mentions, theatre has today added space to its objects of consumption. Moving outside the restricted space within which it was confined for centuries, theatre today can claim and has claimed almost any space the earth provides, natural and artificial, city and country, as potentially part of its domain. An essential part of this process, of course, is the cooperation of the audience in making it work, a cooperation that has always been at the center of the operations of theatre itself. Theatre only began to exist when a performer stood before a group of fellow humans and asked them to see him as something else, as a fictional being, given a new reality by their willingness to look at him in a different way, as a character.

This same process of altering our perception, we now realize, can be applied to any part of our experience, including the space we inhabit. A striking example of this was demonstrated almost forty years ago in an exhibit called *Light Touch* by the New York visual artist Robert Whitman. Whitman created something very close to a traditional theatrical atmosphere by seating his audience as in a theatre but inside a trucking warehouse facing the main warehouse door, which was covered by curtains like a stage opening with an image projected on it. These curtains were then opened to reveal the actual street outside, like a stage setting. According to one of the reports on that performance, the normally banal spectacle of passing traffic was in this manner converted into a strange and fascinating kind of theatre simply by an alteration of perception: "Cars appeared occasionally, framed by the door, as they passed on the street directly outside. Appeared, but appeared transfigured, as if a spell had been cast over them. Details of their shape and movement ordinarily not noticed, leapt out, as if from a numinous aura. It was as if cars were being seen for the first time."[20] Although Whitman's audience remained a traditional passive one, the alteration in their perception indicates clearly how any space can be similarly transfigured, similarly theatricalized. In more recent times, we have seen how this can be done not only with an actual frame, as Whitman demonstrated, but with the frame that the audience itself sustains simply by agreeing to view a space, even one they inhabit, in theatrical terms.

The modern theatre's colonization of space evokes the visions of one of the major pioneers of that development. Nikolai Evreinov, in addition to being the director of one of the first great theatricalizations of public space, the famous *Storming of the Winter Palace* in 1920, was also a major theorist and critic. In a series of books and essays written between 1908 and 1920, he promoted a theatrical view of life in all its aspects. In a typical essay, "Apology for Theatricality," he wrote, "To make a theatre of life is the duty of every artist. . . . The stage must not borrow so much from life as life borrows from the stage."[21] His experiments in "theatre for oneself" distinctly anticipated the forays of *Light Touch* and later immersive work out into the real world. One instance, much in the manner of

Light Touch, was "to sit on a bench in a park or square and look at passing crowds and automobiles," while another looked at more recent work that encourages direct engagement: "To go to a party and behave there 'like a queen.' Like 'a gentleman of importance,' like a 'he-man, and hell-raiser,' like 'a misanthrope,' and so on."[22] He encouraged applying a view of theatre and of stage management to the experience of "walking in the streets, sitting in the restaurants, visiting the boulevards and the stores of Paris or New York or any other place in the world."[23]

In short, Evreinov suggests going a step even beyond the work of Punchdrunk or Rimini Protokoll, and taking upon ourselves their role as organizers and framers of our interaction with the external world. In this way, says Evreinov, we can attain "self-transformation, new feelings, new sensations, new conceptions of the world we live in."[24] Whether the future sees a widespread application of Evreinov's vision or not, experimental theatre's current continuing encroachments upon the real, and particularly its colonization of the real of human space, may be seen as central to the theatre's traditional and ongoing mission. There is now and has always been a desire, through the reflective process of mimesis, to make the human experience in the world more rich, more varied, and more open to experiment and understanding.

Notes

1. Jean Jacquot, *La vie théâtrale au temps de la Renaissance*, quoted in Elie Konigson, *L'espace théâtrale medieval* (Paris, 1975), 95.

2. R.T.R. Clark, *Myth and Symbol in Ancient Egypt* (London: Thames and Hudson, 1959), 65.

3. *Egeria: Diary of a Pilgrimage*, trans. and annotated by George E. Gingras (New York: Newman Press, 1970), 103–5.

4. Gisela Schmidt, *Das Weimarer Liebhabertheater unter Goethes Leitung* (Weimar, 1957), 62–64.

5. Victor Hugo, *Oeuvres completes*, 18 vols. (Paris, 1967), 3:62.

6. Ibid., 63.

7. Wendell Philipps, "Staging a Popular Restaurant," *Theatre Magazine* 5, no. 16:140 (October 1912): 104.

8. Anon., "The Pastoral Players," *Eastward Ho!* 3, no. 1 (May 1885): 429.

9. Quoted in J. L. Syan, *Max Reinhardt* (New York: Cambridge University Press, 1982), 91.

10. Gusti Adler, quoted in George Wellwarth and Alfred Brooks, eds., *Max Reinhardt, 1873–1973: A Centennial Festschrift* (Binghamton, N.Y., 1973), 20.

11. Erika Fischer-Lichte, "Theatre as Festival Play: Ma Reinhardt's Production of *The Merchant of Venice*," in *Venetian Views, Venetian Blinds: English Fantasies*

of Venice, ed. Manfred Pfister and Barbara Schaff (Amsterdam: Rodopi, 1999), 175–79.

12. *Daily Telegraph*, June 4, 1937, *The Sphere* (June 12, 1937), quoted in Robert Shaughnessy, *The Shakespeare Effect: A History of Twentieth-Century Performance* (Houndmills: Palgrave, 2002), 108–9.

13. Ibid.

14. Nikolai Evreinov, *Histoire du théâtre russe*, trans. G. Welter (Paris, 1947), 146.

15. See Howard Giles, "A Brief History of Re-enactment," http://www.event-plan.co.uk/page29.html.

16. Armand Gatti, "Armand Gatti on Time, Place, and the Theatrical Event," trans. Nancy Oakes, *Modern Drama* 25, no. 1 (March 1982): 72.

17. And occasionally even inside a theatre. Mac Wellman's *Crowbar* was presented in 1990 in the then-abandoned Victory Theatre on 42nd Street by En Garde Arts, the leading New York company presenting site-specific work in the 1990s. Today the building, as the New Victory, has been restored to its original theatrical function.

18. See Jennifer Flaherty, "Dreamers and Insomniacs: Audiences in *Sleep No More* and *The Night Circus*," *Comparative Drama* 48, no. 1–2 (Spring/Summer 2014): 135–54.

19. Bert O. States, *Great Reckonings in Little Rooms* (Berkeley: University of California Press, 1985), 40.

20. Bruce Wilshire, *Role Playing and Identity* (Bloomington: Indiana University, 1982), x.

21. Nicolas Evreinoff, *The Theatre in Life*, trans. Alexander L. Nazaroff (New York: Brentano's, 1927), 58.

22. Ibid., 191.

23. Ibid.

24. Ibid., 66.

The Odeon of Pericles

A Tale of the First Athenian Music Hall, the Second Persian Invasion of Greece, Theatre Space in Fifth Century BCE Athens, and the Artifacts of an Empire

Sebastian Trainor

Our story begins around the year 140 CE, on the day when the Roman-era travel writer Pausanias finally reached the Greek city of Athens. One of the items on his to-do list for this city was to take an architectural tour of its theatre district, the precinct of Dionysos. To get to this locale a traveler needed to walk east along the Athenian street of tripods, a road bordered by many small monuments, each of which commemorated a prizewinning theatre production of the past. Pausanias followed this path exactly. And as he came into the hub of the sacred precinct, the first structure of any significant size that he encountered—just before he found the famous Theatre of Dionysos—was a different sort of theatre: a music hall known to history as the Odeon of Pericles (see figure 1). Of it he wrote: "Near the sanctuary and the Theatre of Dionysos is a structure, which is said to be a copy of [the Persian emperor] Xerxes' tent. . . . It has been rebuilt, for the original building was burnt by the Roman general Sulla when he took Athens [in 86 BCE]."[1]

To modern eyes, this encounter is a bit surprising, particularly since, in the twenty-first century, the Odeon no longer exists in any noticeable way.[2] In fact, we get the sense that even Pausanias, in the second century, was somewhat taken aback by the structure. One imagines the ancient tourist trying to puzzle out the historical circumstances that might, 600 years previously, have inspired the Athenians to construct a huge mock-Persian building in the heart of their theatre complex. The present essay attempts this same task of contemplation and interpretation. Its goals are twofold: to uncover the circumstances of the Odeon's construction; and also to illuminate the significance that the original Periclean theatre space would have held for its creators, the Athenians of the fifth century BCE.

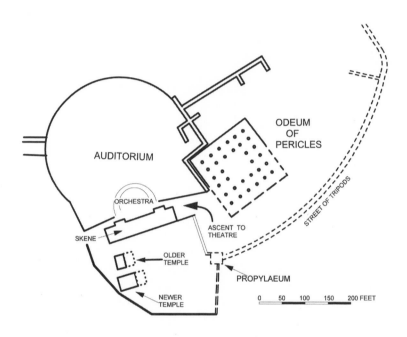

Figure 1. Plan showing the position of the Odeon in relation to the Dionysos Theatre and the Tripod Road. Image created by Todd Canedy based on an illustration in A. W. Pickard-Cambridge's *The Theatre of Dionysus in Athens* (New York: Oxford University Press, 1946), 2. (Modeled on a portion of the fold-out plan of "Old Athens" from *Topographie van Athen* by Walter Judeich [1905]).

Research into the matter suggests that there are three distinct streams of cultural history that commingle in the physical structure of this ancient music hall. This essay explicates each of these briefly, focusing on some startling connections between the (second) Persian invasion of Greece (480–479 BCE) and the overall evolution of the fifth-century BCE Athenian theatre complex. As I argue, the creation of the Odeon in the 440s BCE[3]—a controversial project driven by the efforts of the statesman Pericles—usefully combined three glorious memories of Athenian victory over the Persians into a single architectural expression of the ascendancy of the new Athenian empire. It also, of course, brought into existence a useful public building that was well suited for recitations of poetry accompanied by musical instruments.

The above makes for a fascinating tale, yet the most intriguing feature of this essay is not its central argument. To its author, this investigation creates the impression of a historiographic adventure story. I emphasize this story-ness deliberately, because some key ideas are quite speculative. They are theories from respected classics scholars, to be sure, and are upheld by reasonable probability. But since I am building on a foundation of speculation, the constructions that I offer here should not be mistaken for historical certainties. Indeed, it is partly for this reason that I have composed the essay in a modular fashion. Its various parts can be easily separated from one another so that the reader may pick and choose what to accept as persuasive. If all are embraced, though, the larger picture— the tale of the Odeon's development over a period of several decades— is much greater than the sum of its parts. This is because the story forces us to reconsider some widespread beliefs about the cultural, spatial, and architectural evolution of the early Athenian theatre in general.

Here, I am thinking of the narrative that I learned as an undergraduate, and which still appears in many theatre history textbooks. It begins with the notion that the orchestra (the "dancing place") of the Dionysos Theatre developed from a flat circular area used to thresh grains. The pre-mimetic presentation of devotional dithrambs is said to have taken place on such circles, with an audience fully surrounding the performance area. As time passed, a conveniently nearby storage hut (a proto-*skéné*) became part of the ceremony, causing the circular venue to become directional by re-forming the audience into a half-circle. Soon the "dancing place" was moved to the base of a hill to give spectators better sightlines. Later developments then improved the hillside seating or the dramatic impact of the background.[4]

This easily digestible tale of cultural progress emphasizes the agrarian and religious origins of Western theatrical space. At one time, I took it for gospel. Yet after investigating the historical and political circumstances that led to the construction of the Athenian music hall in the fifth century BCE, I find myself forced to discard that orderly narrative and to completely rethink the sociohistorical significances of each step in the architectural evolution of Athens' celebrated Dionysos Theatre. This opening of a new critical perspective on a familiar topic is an unexpected consequence that gives the present investigation of the Periclean Odeon some equally unexpected gravity. Ultimately, the story that develops in these pages offers an alternative narrative for the physical evolution of a foundational performance space of our Western theatrical past.

Some Preliminaries: The Odeon and the Acropolis

As theatre scholars have rarely considered the Odeon of Pericles, it may benefit from a basic introduction here.[5] This structure was a very large, square, wooden building—nearly two hundred feet per side—that stood at the southeastern foot of the Athenian Acropolis for over 700 years (from ca. 443 BCE until the Herulian sack of Athens in 267 CE).[6] It was adjacent to the east entrance of the Theatre of Dionysos, and it was, itself, also a type of theatre. The name Odeon derives from the Greek "ode," meaning song. The building was, literally, "a place for song"—but more colloquially, it was a music hall. The ancient biographer/historian Plutarch tells us that inside of the original building we would find many seats

Figure 2. Drawing of an ancient Athenian coin (presumed to be a theatre ticket) showing the Odeon of Pericles and found during the excavation of that building's site. From "Το Ωιδειον του Περκλεους" in Αρχαιολογικη Εφημερις *1914*, p. 147 (public domain).

and many pillars.[7] Excavations done in the early twentieth century revealed the Odeon's foundations, confirming that the structure was supported by ninety internal pillars, arranged in nine rows of ten. Exteriorly, the building was distinguished by its exotic pyramidal roof, which gave it an un-Greek look to ancient commentators.[8]

This one-of-a-kind music hall was constructed at the time of a major Athenian building campaign that commenced around the year 440 BCE. The energetic beautification of Athens with new monuments was an innovative civic project that had been championed by the statesman Pericles. His program created many of the landmarks that we associate with the Acropolis today (the Parthenon and the Propylaea, most famously). Yet it is uncertain whether the Odeon was actually a part of the municipally funded project. It was definitely built at the same time as the other monuments, but the Odeon has always been very strongly associated with Pericles as an individual, even from the moment when it was first constructed. It is quite possible that he paid for its creation personally.[9]

During the first century of its existence, the Odeon served three main functions. First, it was a music hall. It was in this venue that the Panathenaic musical competition took place each year.[10] Second, it served as the location for the *proagon* of the dramatic competition of the annual City Dionysia. The *proagon* was a pre-festival ceremony during which the dramatists, who would be competing in the Dionysos Theatre in the days ahead, introduced their actors and the basic scenarios of their works to an assembly of judges, notables, and honored guests.[11] Most of the time, though, the Athenians used the space as a law court.[12]

Speaking generally, the music hall was put to use by the Athenians whenever they needed a large, sheltered, multi-purpose room. But even as we acknowledge this, let us also note that the building simultaneously served a much greater symbolic purpose. The Odeon, as I argue, was conceived to be more monumental than functional. Its architecture, its location, and possibly even the wood from which it was built sent a message that was of great significance to fifth-century BCE Athenians. To interpret that message—and situate it within the history of Athenian theatre practice—is the task of the remainder of this essay.

Part One: The Driftwood of Salamis

To advance the story it is necessary to turn back the clock a few decades from the era of the Odeon's construction and a few centuries from Pausanias' encounter with it. The date is now August of 480 BCE. The three hundred Spartans have made their last stand in the mountain pass of

Thermopylae. No Greek military force remains between the overwhelming invasion army led by the Persian emperor Xerxes and that army's primary objective: the total destruction of the city of Athens. Knowing that this irresistible force was approaching, the Athenians evacuated their polis—transporting all that could be carried to the nearby island of Salamis where, as the ancient historian Herodotus tells us, they hoped the "wooden wall" of their navy would keep them safe.[13]

Soon Xerxes had indeed razed their entire city. Athens' temples, public buildings, and private homes were all pulled down or burned.[14] Shortly after this, Xerxes' navy—more than three times the size of the opposing Greek fleet—positioned itself for the final annihilation of Athenian resistance that was to be the inevitable result of the impending sea battle. To have an excellent view of his victory, Xerxes placed himself on a hilltop overlooking the contested waters. However, due to the famous trick of the Athenian admiral Themistocles, the presumed Persian triumph was semi-miraculously transformed into a resounding defeat.[15]

Aeschylus, the Athenian dramatist, fought as a hoplite marine in this decisive battle. An eyewitness account of the ship-to-ship fighting appears in his tragedy, *The Persians*:

> The Ships of the Greeks, with perfect plan and order, came
> Around [the Persians] in a circle and struck, and hulls of ships
> Were overturned; and the sea no longer was visible,
> Filled as it was with shipwrecks . . .[16]

Yet all this wreckage of ships, if we can believe a later historical source, was not left to drift away. The floating timber was a precious resource, and it seems that it was captured by the Athenians and used to rebuild parts of their ruined city. The Roman architect Vitruvius (writing some 400 years later) reveals the fate of some of it. While describing the Theatre of Dionysos in Athens, he informs his readers that, when they exited this theatre, they would immediately encounter "the music-hall which Themistocles . . . roofed with the yards and masts of ships captured from the Persians."[17] That is, upon exiting the Theatre of Dionysos, any visitor to ancient Athens would immediately find another Greek theatre—the Odeon—that may literally have been built out of Xerxes' lost navy.

The idea that the Athenian music hall was made out of the Persian wreckage demands a certain imaginative generosity. For one thing, today we know that the building was definitely not erected by Themistocles—the fleet admiral and leading Athenian politician at the time of Salamis (479 BCE)—as Vitruvius claimed. Rather, the Odeon was built approximately thirty-five years later (ca. 443 BCE) by Themistocles' political successor, Pericles, who dominated Athenian policy during the next generation. A question therefore arises: If the music hall really was roofed with Persian timber, where was that timber kept for three decades while it waited to serve this purpose?

The noted American philologist and antiquities scholar James T. Allen, in a 1941 article, suggests that the lumber spent three decades as part of the wooden seating structure of the evolving Dionysos Theatre of the 470s, 460s, and 450s. When the seating for this theatre was improved and integrated into the slope of the Acropolis during the 440s, the valuable wood then became available for other projects. In this way, he claims, the actual Persian timber may have come to be incorporated into the new Periclean Odeon.[18]

It is impossible to say whether this presumed résumé of the Persian timber constitutes the real historical truth. The notion is a conjecture that can never be proved. Nonetheless, merely considering Allen's proposition can help theatre historians redress some of the misconceptions we may hold concerning theatrical performances in Golden Age Athens. For one thing, his idea that the "masts and spars" spent three decades as part of the bleachers (the *ikria*, in Greek) of the Dionysos Theatre awakens us to the fact that a freestanding wooden *ikria* really was the seating structure for that theatre during the fifth century BCE. (That part of Allen's argument is not speculative at all.) And for us to have some knowledge of the *ikria*, in turn, makes us realize that the Golden Age Athenian dramatists—Aeschylus, Sophocles, Euripides, and their competitors—did not write for an enormous semicircular stone performance venue, with a capacity of 15,000-plus, and a stage that included an elaborate architectural façade. (*That* theatre would not exist until the following century.) Rather, the theatre these writers knew was both more exclusive and less elaborate. It had rectilinear wooden bleachers, it accommodated only a few thousand citizens at best, and it had no permanent scene building (*skéné*, in Greek) to contain the stage space.[19]

The small scale and the absent *skéné* of the early fifth-century BCE Dionysos Theatre are both important background details for my soon-to-be-drawn portrait of the then (in the 470s) soon-to-be built Odeon. Allen's idea concerning the Persian timber, however, will serve as an even more crucial element for the picture's construction. Therefore, for the argumentative purposes of this essay, his hypothesis that the *ikria* (and later the Odeon) was built of conquered and recycled ships is embraced here as a foundational idea.

Part Two: The Tent of Xerxes

At the start of this essay we were introduced to the Athenian music hall by Pausanias, who stood contemplating the "structure which is said to be a copy of Xerxes' tent."[20] To perceive it more clearly, our Roman-era traveler might have consulted a recent work that may have been well known to him: Plutarch's *Life of Pericles*. The biography of the Athenian politician had been written a few decades before Pausanias' own grand tour, and enjoyed wide popularity in Greece as well as Rome. Reading it, Pausanias would have realized that the "structure" was, in fact, an odeon—a hall for recitations accompanied by musical instruments. As Plutarch describes it: "The Odeon, or music-room, was in its interior full of seats and ranges of pillars, and outside had its roof made to slope and descend from one single point at the top. It was constructed, we are told, in imitation of the King of Persia's pavilion; this by Pericles' order."[21]

Significantly, both Plutarch and Pausanias record that this notable structure imitated the tent of the Persian emperor Xerxes, who, from the shade provided by that structure, witnessed the decisive defeat of the Persian navy in the summer of 480 BCE. After that catastrophe, as Herodotus tells us, Xerxes experienced a sudden desire to return home. He abandoned his ostentatious pavilion to the use of Mardonius, his brother-in-law, who stayed behind in Greece as commander of the now stranded invasion army. One year later the luxurious command tent was captured by the Greeks after the final defeat of the Persian infantry.[22]

In a compelling but often overlooked article of 1944 entitled "The Tent of Xerxes and the Greek Theater," the Swedish American archaeologist Oscar Broneer argued that the captured tent was then brought to (the ruins of) Athens and displayed in the precinct of Dionysos.[23] Broneer asserts that the tent itself was used in such early theatrical performances as Phrynichus' *Phoenician Women* (476 BCE) and Aeschylus' *The Persians* (472 BCE). Especially eye-opening are his observations concerning the term used in Greek to refer to this Persian tent: "*skéné*." This was an exotic new word at the time of these dramas. In fact, the word "*skéné*" makes its first recorded appearance in the Greek language in Aeschylus' aforementioned play. As Broneer explains, after the 470s this word would become "the common designation for a military tent" to be used throughout all later Greek literature.[24] Theatre scholars, of course, already know the term "*skéné*" as referring to the not-yet-invented (at the time of *The Persians*) architectural façade of the evolving Dionysos Theatre. For Broneer, the two meanings of this word—both entering the language at the same historical moment—form convincing proof that the façade of the emperor's tent was the prototype for the permanent scene building of the Athenian theatre.[25]

Yet it is Broneer's more general assertion, that the imperial tent was brought to and displayed in Athens, which most interests us in relation to the goals of this investigation of the Periclean Odeon. Given the persuasiveness with which the archaeologist constructs his case, the circumstantial evidence that he presents, and the absence of any alternative theory regarding the fate of that marvelous object, it is difficult not to embrace his judgment in the matter. For the present study, then, only a slight corollary refocusing of Broneer's argument is needed—one that shifts the view away from the Dionysos Theatre and onto the Odeon. Why, I ask, would the Athenians choose to create a civic building that was "a copy of Xerxes' tent" if that notable war trophy were not already somehow connected to their city?

Part Three: *The Persians* of Aeschylus

Pausanias has now shone as much light as he can on the world's first music hall. Leaving him behind, we continue this study by transporting ourselves to the Athenian City Dionysia of 472 BCE. At this date the Odeon had not yet been built. Nonetheless, the festival's dramatic competition in that year is crucial for the illumination of the building's future significance. It was on this occasion that the salvaged timber of Salamis and the captive tent of Xerxes may first have been pressed into active service by the young Pericles. At this particular Dionysia, at the age of twenty, the future "first citizen of Athens" served as producer/*choregos* for the début presentation of Aeschylus' *The Persians*. This was his first public act for which any record survives.[26]

The dramatic action of Aeschylus' play exalts the near-miraculous Athenian naval victory at Salamis. For the Athenian spectators in the audience that event had occurred only eight years prior, and many of them had been actual combatants. Yet Aeschylus presents the consequences of the battle from the Persian point of view. His play is set in Xerxes' homeland, and all of its characters are Persian. For them the tale is a tragedy; for the Athenian audience it is self-congratulatory.

The Persians was part of the newly reinstated competition of the City Dionysia, Athens' spring festival dedicated not only to Dionysos but also to Athenian achievement more generally. Embracing one of Broneer's ideas helps us to visualize the occasion. Let us suppose that there, set up at the rear of the orchestra of the developing Dionysos Theatre, stood gaudy material proof of that aforementioned achievement: the field tent

of Xerxes himself. Aeschylus might even have written with this war trophy in mind. (He repeatedly emphasizes the gilded luxury of the Persian
army in his chorus opening song.) If used in the production, the opulence
of the emperor's tent must have made a striking contrast to the barren-
ness of Athens itself, still dotted with uncleared ruins.[27]

As we now know, in 472 BCE there was neither stone seating nor *skéné*
associated with the original Theatre of Dionysos. *The Persians* is the earliest surviving Greek drama, belonging to an era when the Athenian performance space was actively evolving. The few thousand spectators lucky
enough to attend this premiere sat in an *ikria*—which, it seems, may have
been constructed of timber salvaged from the invading ships that these
same individuals had destroyed at Salamis. It is also plausible that they sat
facing the fancy Persian tent that was captured at the war's final battle. In
this way the performance, before it even began, may already have incorporated two potent relics of the recent war.

Following this scenario, Pericles' chorus of Persian "elders" now enters the playing area, dressed in their outlandish costumes.[28] As they ar-
rive in the orchestra, they pass before the famous tent, representing the
royal palace in Persia, singing:

> We are the ones whom the Persians gone
> To the land of Greece left behind . . .[29]

For many months they have awaited news of the great conquest. At
last, a Messenger comes to them. This role was likely to have been performed by Aeschylus himself.[30] The tragedian was fifty-two years old at
the time, famous throughout Attica not only for his writing, but also
for his valor as a soldier. The Messenger begins to recount the disas-
trous naval defeat:

> I did not hear an account from others, I was there,
> Persians, and can tell details of the disaster.[31]

In truth, the poet had been there. He did fight, and could tell the details.
The first of these was the beginning of the Persian nightmare:

> A man, a Greek, arrived from the Athenian camp
> And spoke to Xerxes words to this effect . . .[32]

Hearing these lines every member of the audience would know that "a
man, a Greek" meant Themistocles specifically. Perhaps they even turned
about on their Persian ship-timber benches to note him. Far from modest, Themistocles may have preened himself while the tragedian recounted

the cunning lie by which he, Themistocles, triggered the Persian defeat and became the principal hero of Salamis.[33]

On that day in the spring of 472, in a prototypical theatre space that may literally have been constructed from war artifacts, Aeschylus and Pericles re-created for the Athenian veterans the greatest moments of their lives: those in which they brought about the miracle of Salamis. At the end of the competition the judges awarded *The Persians* the first prize for tragedy. This decision, I propose, may have been partly compelled by the potent construction of the venue itself: by its incorporation of the Tent of Xerxes, and by the judges' own awareness that they were seated upon planks of the defeated Persian ships as the old Persian king lamented the fate of his navy:

> . . . all this country's
> Three-banked ships are lost,
> Ships no longer ships.[34]

Part Four: The Odeon of Pericles

One final time we adjust the clock, fast-forwarding three decades to 443 BCE. Approximately. We are not certain of the exact year in which our new focal event—the construction of the Odeon—takes place. It is certain, though, that both Pericles and Athens have by this date arrived at the highest plateau of their political influence. Athens has become an empire in its own right, and Pericles is now its most influential citizen. The foundations of the new Parthenon have recently been put in place, but it will be twelve more years before the temple is completed. We are at the front end of a very busy era of Athenian civic beautification.[35]

So far this study has embraced two key conjectures that may (or may not) be historically accurate. One is the idea that the Odeon of Pericles was built in formal imitation of the famous Tent of Xerxes that is believed to have been on display in Athens for three decades. The other is that this new tent-imitating building was constructed of recycled Persian ship timber that had spent thirty years as part of the seating structure for the annual city Dionysia. There is, however, an important question that has not yet been discussed: Why was the Odeon built at all? In response to this, three distinct explanations suggest themselves. They are by no means mutually exclusive, but they do derive from substantially different viewpoints, one overtly political, another purely practical, and the last relating to Pericles' own personal history.

First is the overtly political explanation. For insight we turn to a small textual fragment that has survived from the (lost) satirical play *The Thracian Women* by the Athenian comic playwright Cratinus:

> we see here
> The squill-pate Pericles appear,
> Since ostracism time, he's laid aside his head,
> And wears the new Odeon in its stead.[36]

This bit of Old Comedy is believed to have been written in 443 BCE.[37] It is the earliest reference to the Odeon that still exists, and from its own testimony we know it was written when the tent-like structure was "new." The passage makes a joke about the elongated onion-shape (a squill is a type of wild onion) of the head of the middle-aged and politically radical statesman, Pericles. The Odeon's cupola apparently suggested to Cratinus that a miniature version of the recently completed structure would serve as a good comic hat for the portrait-mask that would represent Pericles onstage.[38] Yet if we move past the comedic surface of the sight gag and consider the phrase "since ostracism time" more carefully, we find that this particular fragment of the fragment implies a bit more about the overall cultural meaning of the new music hall.

Specifically, the reference to ostracism directly connects the contemporary significance of the music hall to a life-and-death political struggle that took place between Pericles (leader of the popular/democratic party) and his longtime ideological antagonist, Thucydides (the son of Milesias and leader of the Athenian conservative/aristocratic party, not the third-century BCE historian).[39] In 443 BCE, these two prominent citizens locked horns to see which would successfully ostracize the other. Their quarrel had arisen over the appropriate use of revenue from the Athenian empire—money paid to Athens as "tribute" by less potent Greek cities and intended for military expenditures against the Persians. Pericles felt that since a final peace with the Persians had been formally concluded in 449, the revenue should now be used to clean up the old ruins and stimulate the local economy by employing much of the Athenian population in construction projects. Thucydides vigorously disagreed. In the end, when the potsherds were counted, Pericles had won the vote and Thucydides was ostracized. The Odeon, as some specialists have argued, was probably the first structure of that extended civic building project to be completed. It began the step-by-step transformation of Athens into an architectural marvel, which strove to convince visitors that this city deserved to rule over all the world.[40] If this was indeed (a part of) the goal, then we may take the Cratinus fragment not merely as satire, but as an apt metaphor: Pericles was wearing the Odeon as a hat because it was his crowning achievement, a diadem to signify the political victory at "ostracism time," which launched the new program of civic beautification and architectural imperialism.

I do not, however, wish to lose sight of the Athenians' more quotidian building needs while imagining their imperial aspirations. One indisputable fact is that the Odeon did exist. It was most definitely used by Athenian citizens for purposes other than exterior display and its existence did have a practical explanation in addition to its political explanation. So on a simply utilitarian level it is easy to suppose that, if the building's presumed model, the wonderful Tent of Xerxes, had indeed been in Athens for over thirty years (ever since its supposed first appearance in the Dionysos Theatre in the 470s), then that tent had probably become less wonderful than it once was. It also seems likely that a sheltered structure of such large dimensions would have been put to some practical municipal use. In 443, then, the tent might have been in need of replacement. I propose that it was replaced with a more permanent structure: the Odeon. The replacement would, quite reasonably, copy the appearance of the original, as the original war artifact was of great symbolic value to the Athenians. And so long as the proposed Periclean building program included an improved seating structure for the Dionysos Theatre anyway, what building material could possibly be more appropriate to memorialize the famous tent than the timber salvaged from that other Athenian victory over the Persian invaders?

However practical the construction of the Odeon may have been for Athens at large, and however necessary it may have been for an imperial power to have an awe-inspiring capital, still, the most edifying way for us to explain the building of the new music hall is in relation to Pericles' own personal history and agenda for the future. He built the structure "seeking acclaim," says Plutarch.[41] The monument is, was, and always has been associated with this particular statesman very directly. It is known to history with his name attached: "the Odeon of Pericles." One specialist has argued that he even paid for the construction of the building exclusively from his own personal fortune as a gift to the city, rather than making it part of the concurrent municipally funded building project.[42] What, one wonders, was his personal stake in the matter?

If the conjectures that have been embraced throughout this essay are correct, then the new Odeon's form and construction material can also be viewed, in addition to commemorating the Athenian victory at Salamis, as also commemorating one of Pericles' own personal victories: the prizewinning production of *The Persians* at the Dionysia of 472 (see figure 3). The cultural importance of that triumph should not be undervalued. Since Pericles was the producer/*choregos* for the occasion, the glory of the win belonged to him much more than to his playwright/collaborator Aeschylus.[43] Indeed, for Pericles the personal significance of the win at the Dionysia may have been further enhanced by the fact that it was this

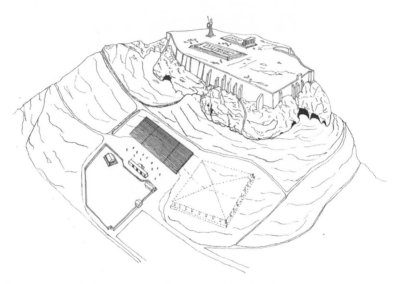

Figure 3. Speculative reconstruction of the Athenian theatron of the 450s BCE. Note the wooden bleachers, the site of the soon-to-be-constructed Odeon, and the current state of development of the Acropolis, which features, at this time, only the brand new statue of Athena by Pheidias. Image created by Desiree Sanchez Meineck as illustration for an article by Peter Meineck, "The Embodied Space: Performance and Visual Cognition at the Fifth Century Athenian Theatre," *New England Classical Journal* 39, no. 1 (2012). Courtesy of Desiree Sanchez Meineck and Peter Meineck.

event that had launched him into public life. What I especially wish to note, though, is that the production of *The Persians* makes a clear historical connection between Pericles as an individual and the Persian artifacts that seem to have played a role in the play's performance—artifacts which were now (as we suppose) being used to create Pericles' Odeon.

All of this suggests that we must read (at least) a double meaning in the architecture of the new music hall. On the one hand the structure is identified with military victory over Persia; on the other it is linked with the personal victory of Pericles as *choregos*. The new music hall then creates an equation between the previously separate significances of the two events: Periclean leadership equals victory over the Persians. It is a sort of architectural equivocation, masterfully deployed by the man who caused the Odeon to be built. Whether Pericles paid for this monument out of pocket, or successfully advocated that the state should bear the construction cost, becomes a moot point. What matters is that it was made of war artifacts and that it was created through Pericles' personal intervention.

In these ways, then, the construction of the Odeon might be interpreted as a deliberate effort by the (then fifty-one-year-old) politician of 443 BCE to associate himself with the miraculous Athenian victories over the Persians in 480–479 BCE. As the actual veterans of Salamis began to disappear from public life, Pericles may even have usurped in the public imagination the heroic credit belonging to the admiral Themistocles. Thus, Pericles might have made himself, retroactively, into the hero of the Persian War who emerged victorious over Xerxes. And he may have accomplished this "monumental" sleight-of-hand at the exact moment when his new building program strove to develop the city of Athens into an architecturally magnificent capital for a growing empire.

So, in answer to one of the guiding questions of this study—What significance did the original Odeon hold for the Athenians of 443 BCE?—the following three ideas emerge. First, the structure "which is said to be a copy of Xerxes' tent" commemorates and celebrates the Athenian triumph over the Persian invasion. Second, the exotic nature of this monument assured the Athenian citizenry that Athens was now a great imperial power in its own right, ready and able to supplant the much older empire of the Persians. And third, both of these conditions had come about through the genius of Pericles, who built the monument out of war artifacts that were already associated with one of his own political achievements.

Conclusion: The Narrative of Theatre and Space

In this essay's introduction I acknowledged the unexpectedness of the conclusion to which I *had been led* by the process of the investigation, and at which point I have now arrived. I hardly perceived the changes as they occurred, but when I finally felt that I understood something of the Odeon, I found, also, that my understanding of the sociopolitical function of the Athenian theatre complex in general had been completely reprogrammed.

As a final rehearsal of this point let us suppose that, in the sixth century BCE, Athenian theatre practices really did originate in devotional rituals. Let us also suppose that, in the beginning, these were enacted on threshing circles. Even granting this, such origins shed only a dim light on the fifth-century BCE Athenian theatre. That is, they shed only a dim light on the actual theatre space belonging to all of the surviving plays of Aeschylus, Sophocles, and Euripides—for in the wake of the complete destruction of Athens by the Persians in 480 BCE, the polis' theatre had to be re-created, literally from the ground up.

After the last of the Persian army was eradicated from Greece, the Athenian theatre clearly underwent a thorough reinvention: both as a cultural activity and as a spatial/architectural entity. The use of the Persian invasion as subject matter; of the Persian ship timbers to build a seating structure; of the emperor's tent as scenery; the later reuse of these war artifacts to create a music hall: these are highly symbolic political acts. If the story that has been pieced together in these pages is correct, then the material performance space that belonged to our earliest surviving plays had very little to do with Dionysos, religious ritual, or the cycle of the harvest, but it had everything to do with proclaiming Athenian cultural dominance and launching the city's imperialist future.

Notes

1. Pausanias, *The Description of Greece*, trans. J. G. Frazer (London: R. Faulder, 1898), 1.20.4.

2. The foundation of the Odeon of Pericles is preserved today as an archeological site, but it does not call much attention to itself.

3. Specialists disagree over the exact construction date for the original Odeon: 450 BCE is the earliest proposal with any claim to credibility, with 437 BCE being the latest. Most promote either 446 or 443 BCE, according to which of the literary evidences they find most persuasive. This essay assumes the date of 443 BCE proposed by James T. Allen (see note 18, below). An overview of the debate is given by Anne Lou Hawkins Robkin (see note 5, below).

4. The work that first introduced me to this evolutionary narrative that leads from threshing circle to Dionysos Theatre is a textbook by B. Donald Grose and O. Franklin Kenworthy, *A Mirror to Life: A History of Western Theatre* (New York: Holt, Rinehart and Winston, 1985), 29–33. Of that particular work there is no newer edition, but a quick survey of more recent textbooks gives variations in Martin Banham, ed., *The Cambridge Guide to Theatre* (Cambridge: Cambridge University Press, 1995), 1086; Kimball King, ed., *Western Drama through the Ages: A Student Reference Guide* (Westport, Conn.: Greenwood Press, 2007), 547; Milly S. Barranger, *Theatre: A Way of Seeing* (Stamford, Conn.: Cengage Learning, 2015), 24; and many others. Yet these are general introductions or reference works. In the specialized scholarly literature pertaining to the Theatre of Dionysos in Athens, one can read a helpful genealogy of the notion of the threshing floor as proto-orchestra in Rush Rehm, *The Play of Space: Spatial Transformation in Greek Tragedy* (Princeton, N.J.: Princeton University Press, 2002), 316n.23. The idea seems to originate in a 1955 article by Annie Dunman Ure, "Threshing Floor or Vineyard," *Classical Quarterly* 5 (1955): 225–30. By 1989 the threshing

floor theory is proffered as being extremely likely by Peter D. Arnott, *Public and Performance in Greek Theatre* (New York: Routledge, 1989), 2–3.

5. The only commentary I have found on the Odeon that originates in the field of theatre studies is a brief treatment in David Wiles, *Tragedy in Athens: Performance Space and Theatrical Meaning* (Cambridge: Cambridge University Press, 1997), 54–55. In the field of classical studies there is greater abundance, but scholarship on the Odeon is still less plentiful than one might hope. In chronological order, some works that deal with the subject in a substantial way are James Turney Allen, "On the Odeum of Pericles and the Periclean Reconstruction of the Theater," *University of California Publications in Classical Archaeology* 1, no. 7 (1941): 173–77; Oscar Broneer, "The Tent of Xerxes and the Greek Theater," *University of California Publications in Classical Archaeology* 1, no. 12 (1944): 305–11; Anne Lou Hawkins Robkin, "The Odeion of Perikles: Some Observations on Its History, Form, and Functions" (PhD diss., University of Washington, 1976); A. L. H. Robkin, "The Odeion of Perikles: The Date of Its Construction and the Periklean Building Program," *Ancient World* 1, no. 1 (1979): 3–12; A. L. H. Robkin, "The Tent of Xerxes and the Odeion of Themistokles: Some Speculations," *The Ancient World* 3, no. 2 (1980): 44–46; Margaret Miller, *Athens and Persia in the Fifth Century BC* (Cambridge: Cambridge University Press, 1997), 218–42; Anthony J. Podlecki, *Perikles and His Circle* (New York: Routledge, 1998), 77–81.

6. The most comprehensive study of the Odeon to date in English is Robkin, "The Odeion of Perikles: Some Observations." Robkin examines each era of this structure's history, starting with its construction in the 440s BCE, through various repairs made over the centuries, to its destruction by fire in 86 BCE and subsequent rebuilding, and then to its final destruction in the sacking of Athens in 267 CE.

7. Plutarch, *The Life of Pericles*, trans. Alan Wardman (Berkeley: University of California Press, 1974), 13.5.

8. Both Pausanias (*Description of Greece*, 1.20.4) and Plutarch, (*Pericles*, 13.5) invoke the Persianness of the Odeon's appearance.

9. Robkin makes a case for Pericles having financed the construction of the Odeon entirely from his personal fortune. See her dissertation "The Odeion of Perikles," 56–60.

10. Plutarch, *Pericles*, 13.5–6.

11. We obtain a fair amount of detail concerning this ceremony from the scholiast preserved in one of the speeches of the fourth-century BCE orator Aeschines. See Aeschines, *Against Ctesiphon*, 67.

12. We know this from a number of ancient references, one of the most prominent being in the parabasis of Aristophanes' play *The Wasps* (1107–1111). For a thorough commentary on the sources cited in notes 10–12 see Robkin, "The Odeion of Perikles: Some Observations," 71–86.

13. Herodotus, *The History of the Persian Wars*, trans. David Grene (Chicago: University of Chicago Press, 1987), 7.140–43.

14. Ibid., 8.50–55.

15. Ibid., 8.74–103.

16. Aeschylus, *The Persians*, trans. Anthony Podlecki (Englewood Cliffs, N.J.: Prentice-Hall, 1970), 417–20.

17. Vitruvius Pollio, *De Architectura*, trans. Ingrid D. Rowland (New York: Cambridge University Press, 1999), 5.9.

18. James Turney Allen, "On the Odeum of Pericles and the Periclean Reconstruction of the Theater," *University of California Publications in Classical Archaeology* 1, no. 7 (1941): 173–77.

19. In the seven decades since Allen's article, there has been a fairly continuous debate among specialists over the size, shape, and construction of the *ikria* of the fifth-century Athenian theatre of Dionysos. Arguments in favor of a rectilinear wooden structure date from Carlo Anti, *Teatri greci arcaici da Minosse a Pericle* (Padua, 1947). One of his most helpful (to this essay) illustrations was reproduced in the second edition of Margarete Bieber's *History of the Greek and Roman Theater* (Princeton, N.J.: Princeton University Press, 1961), fig. 229. Later, Anti's arguments found a new champion in Elizabeth Gebhard, "The Form of the Orchestra in the Early Greek Theater," *Hesperia* 43, no. 4 (1974). A useful survey of the first half-century of the debate is given by Clifford Ashby, "The Case for the Rectangular/Trapezoidal Orchestra," *Theatre Research International* 13 (1988). As for recent scholarship that envisions the Dionysos Theatre as rectilinear, wooden, and able to accommodate only a few thousand spectators, see Eric Csapo, "The Men Who Built the Theaters: Theatropolai, Theatronai, and Arkhitektones," in P. Wilson, ed., *The Greek Theatre and Festivals: Documentary Studies* (Oxford: Oxford University Press, 2007); and David Roselli, *Theater of the People: Spectators and Society in Ancient Athens* (Austin: University of Texas Press, 2011).

20. Pausanias, *Description of Greece*, 1.20.4.

21. Plutarch, "The Life of Pericles," 13.5.

22. Herodotus, *The History*, 9.82. See also 8.100–102. For an analysis of exactly how ornate the imperial tent was, see Broneer, "The Tent of Xerxes and the Greek Theater," 306n.5.

23. Broneer, "The Tent of Xerxes," 305–11. See previous note for full citation.

24. Ibid., 311.

25. Ibid., 309–10.

26. Anthony J. Podlecki, "Introduction," in Aeschylus, *The Persians* (Englewood Cliffs, N.J.: Prentice-Hall, 1970), 9.

27. After the Persians sacked Athens in 480 BCE, the Athenians did not rebuild their temples and monuments, nor even clear these ruins from their city. This behavior kept faith with the so-called "Oath of Plataea," supposedly sworn by all of the Greeks just before the final battle against the Persians (in 479 BCE). One of the details of this oath was that, if the Greeks were victorious in the battle, they would not rebuild any of the sacred structures that the invaders had destroyed. Rather, these were to be deliberately left in a destroyed state to serve as reminders of the invaders' barbarity and impiety. For more details of the pledge see Lycurgus, *Against Leocrates*, 80–81, and Diodorus, *Library of History*, 11.29.2–3. Among the Athenians the oath would hold for three decades—until the final peace with the Persians was concluded in ca. 449 BCE. After this the Athenians apparently

felt themselves to be released from the vow and began their major rebuilding projects of the 440s. For more on this subject see Plutarch's *Life of Pericles*, especially chapters 12, 13, and 17.

28. Persian stage characters in ancient Athens wore such outrageous (to Athenian eyes) things as trousers, for instance. For a thorough discussion of what is known of Athenian choral costume via the iconographic record, see Oliver Taplin and Rosie Wyles, eds., *The Pronomos Vase and Its Context* (New York: Oxford University Press, 2010).

29. Aeschylus, *The Persians*, 1–2.

30. That Aeschylus took this particular role is my own speculation. It is known that, until such time as Sophocles added a third actor (ca. 460 BCE), Athenian tragedies involved only two principal performers—with one of these being the author himself. For more detail see A. W. Pickard-Cambridge, *The Dramatic Festivals of Athens* (Oxford: Oxford University Press, 1968), 130–32; and Gerald F. Else, "The Case of the Third Actor," *Transactions and Proceedings of the American Philological Association* 76 (1945): 1–10.

31. Aeschylus, *The Persians*, 266–67.

32. Ibid., 355–56.

33. The presence of Themistocles at the performance is likely but not definite. This politician/hero's popularity was in serious decline as the 470s BCE drew to a close. It is known that he was ostracized sometime between 476 and 471. Many specialists believe he was still in Athens in 472, and that the presentation of *The Persians* by his political allies Aeschylus and Pericles was part of a campaign to restore his popularity. See, for instance, Anthony Podlecki, *The Life of Themistocles: A Critical Survey of the Literary and Archeological Evidence* (Montreal: McGill-Queen's University Press, 1975), 34–37.

34. Aeschylus, *The Persians*, 677–79.

35. On the hegemony of Athens, the rise of the Athenian Empire, or the emergence of Pericles as politically foremost among the Athenians, see Podlecki, *Perikles and His Circle*, especially chapters 5–7. On the date of the Odeon's construction, or on the Athenian building program of the 440s and 430s in general, see Robkin, "The Odeion of Perikles: Some Observations," 36–51, or Allen, "On the Odeum of Pericles," 173–77.

36. This fragment of Cratinus appears in Plutarch's *Life of Pericles* at 12.3. Because of his unusual "squill-headed" physiognomy, Pericles had a habit of wearing his military helmet whenever he appeared in public. A further passage from Plutarch's study of the statesman is more informative on this subject: "His personal appearance was unimpeachable, except that his head was rather long and out of due proportion. For this reason the images of him, almost all of them, wear helmets, because the artists, as it would seem, were not willing to reproach him with deformity" (3.1–4).

37. This date of composition is based on the assumption that the ostracism referred to in the fragment was that of Pericles' political rival Thucydides, known to have occurred in 443 BCE. This interpretation is accepted by many, but not by all, classics scholars who have considered the subject. Opponents of this choice

of date note that "ostracism time" came around every year, and that Thucydides is not specifically named in the surviving text. They offer other dates of composition for Cratinus' play ranging from 450 to 437 BCE, according to their beliefs regarding when the Odeon was "new." For more on the ostracism of Thucydides, see Allen, "On the Odeum," 174. On the construction date of the Odeon see above, note 3.

38. On portrait masks in Old Comedy see Pickard-Cambridge, *Dramatic Festivals*, 218–19.

39. My assumption that the fragment's mention of "ostracism" refers specifically to the ostracism of Thucydides follows convention, but it is not universally accepted among classics scholars. See note 37, above. See also Robkin, "The Odeion of Perikles: Some Observations," 36–41.

40. On this subject see Miller, *Athens and Persia in the Fifth Century BC*, 239–42. In her discussion Miller cites one of the speeches of the fourth-century Athenian orator Isocrates, which is worth reproducing here: "And of our generation, who does not remember this, that the democracy so adorned the city with temples and public buildings that even now visitors think that she is worthy of ruling not only the Greeks but everyone else as well" (Isocrates, 7.66).

41. Plutarch, *Pericles*, 13.11.

42. Robkin, "The Odeion of Perikles: Some Observations," 56–60.

43. On this subject, see Peter Wilson, *The Athenian Institution of the Khoregia* (Cambridge: Cambridge University Press, 2000), especially chapters 4–6.

The Eyeline of Orestes

Exploring the Dramaturgy of Civic
Space in the Greek Theatre

Samuel T. Shanks

Writing about Greek theatre is notoriously hazardous. Solid physical evidence is scarce, and we only have a handful of plays to represent the entire period. Nevertheless, the Greeks continue to be of critical importance to twenty-first-century theatre academics and practitioners. Greek theatre is featured prominently in nearly every "Introduction to Theatre" and theatre history course, and adaptations and revival productions appear consistently in our production seasons. Therefore, despite the challenges of working in this corner of the field, we must continue to reengage this small but disproportionally important body of evidence to see if our ever-evolving array of critical tools can bring new insights to our understanding of the period.

Naturally, this requires us to operate more theoretically than we would if we were working in a more recent period. Our analyses, which rest upon these more abstractly derived theories, will subsequently be shakier and more subject to later revision. Yet such theoretical contributions may nevertheless provide useful insights into how these enduring classics may have operated in their own time, and how modern adaptations and revivals might best bring them to life in ours.

In this brief article I examine a number of important moments from *The Oresteia* with a particular eye toward what I describe as the play's "dramaturgy of space." My analysis of this spatial dramaturgy is informed by prior scholarship that has helped us to understand the sociological position of the Greek theatre structure as a civic space within Greek society, rather than simply a site of entertainment.

Undergirding my discussion of *The Oresteia*'s dramaturgy of space is an ongoing analysis of the physical layout of the classical Theatre of Dionysus at Athens, the trilogy's original performance venue. Noteworthy studies of the use of space in the Greek theatre have preceded this one, and my work is built in part upon the accomplishments of these prior scholars. Oliver Taplin's 1977 book *The Stagecraft of Aeschylus* was groundbreaking in its exhaustive analysis of the spatial implications built into the play-texts themselves; *Tragedy in Athens: Performance Space and Theatrical Meaning*, by David Wiles, takes a sophisticated and highly nuanced approach to analyzing the civic and religious dynamics of Greek tragedies.[1] My analysis of *The Oresteia* operates somewhere between these two studies, maintaining much of the pragmatic flavor of Taplin's study while being heavily informed by more recent generations of scholars, like Wiles, whose attention to the cultural context from which the plays arose has proved so valuable.

Further informing my own analysis are recent insights into human perception emerging from neuroscience research, which are increasingly being utilized by scholars in the humanities in much the same way that research from psychology informed the psychoanalytical approaches to criticism in the mid- to late twentieth century. Often loosely categorized under the umbrellas of cognitive studies or cognitive science, this research emerges from a remarkably diverse array of scientific disciplines. The value in bringing the emerging perspectives of cognitive studies to bear on an analysis of ancient theatrical productions comes from our understanding of the universality of many of the mechanisms of human perception across cultures and eras. Social customs and religious attitudes have changed dramatically in the nearly 2,500 years since the first production of *The Oresteia*, but the anatomy of the human eye, and the neurological structure that connects it to the mind, has not. We may have to continually hedge our statements regarding the precise layout of the classical Theatre of Dionysus at Athens, but we can discuss with great confidence the perceptual mechanisms that allowed the spectators to imaginatively transform the scenery into the palace of the House of Atreus.

Although the kind of cultural contextualization that has become such a familiar part of our scholarship over the past few decades implicitly increases our focus on the spectatorial versus the textual aspects of theatre, an analysis rooted in cognitive studies will tend to focus on spectatorship in a far more literal way. Thus my analysis of spatial dramaturgy will necessarily include more than just the kind of textually based spatial cues that Taplin focuses on. If we are to consider the hypothetical cognitive perception of classical Greek spectators, then the overall layout of the physical space in which the productions occurred becomes of critical importance. The relative location of the spectators to the performance space, to the other spectators, and to the rest of the polis all have the ability to alter the perceptual process. Considered together, the material arrangement of all these elements within physical space creates a kind of "architecture of perception" that has the power to shape each spectator's perception of the theatrical events.[2] The nature of human subjectivity will ensure that perception will always remain a highly idiosyncratic event, yet it is nevertheless possible to analyze the ways in which highly skilled playwrights such as Aeschylus crafted their plays dramaturgically to suit the perceptual dynamics of the specific performance spaces for which they were destined.

The Dramaturgy of Space

Dramaturgy is an area of inquiry that often overlooks the use of space. There are good reasons for this, as the division of labor in the modern theatre typically cedes the control of spatial matters to the directing and design staffs. In fact, many directing and design students are encouraged to pay little or no attention to a playwright's stage directions.

However, it would be a grave error to completely ignore the dramaturgy of space, particularly when looking at plays that were written with specific performance conditions in mind. When writing for a known space, playwrights frequently make dramaturgical choices that take advantage of the particular spatial characteristics of the known space in which their work will be performed. A straightforward example would be the prologue to Shakespeare's *Henry V*, in which the character labeled simply as "Chorus" asks:

> Can this cockpit hold
> the vasty fields of France: Or may we cram
> Within this wooden O the very casques
> That did affright the air at Agincourt?
> (*Henry V*: Act I, Prologue)

The references to "cockpits" and "wooden O's" in this famously metatheatrical speech help to stake out the boundaries of the spatial dramaturgy of the play. In describing his theatre as a "cockpit," Shakespeare's Chorus reminds the spectators of the Globe's decidedly humble and marginalized location at the vice-ridden outskirts of the city;[3] in describing his performance space as a "wooden O," Shakespeare creates a sense of theatrical community that encompasses the performers and the spectators alike, and encourages everyone involved to shift their eyeline from the stage to the larger structure of the Globe theatre, with its numerous "circles" of galleries and rooflines.

These references, along with the subsequent metatheatrical references by the Shakespearean Chorus throughout the play, alter the spectators' perception of the performance space in important ways. When it comes to visual perception, much of our cognitive architecture is focused on the identification of the borders between objects. As such, our ability to visually identify and cognitively process these borders is rooted in the layout of the rods and cones of our retinas and extends to the layout of the neurons to which they are connected. Often these borders are more physically defined (e.g., where an actor's hand ends and where her prop begins) while other borders are more metaphorical (e.g., upstage vs. downstage), but our cognitive handling of each instance remains nearly identical.[4]

Shakespeare's reference to the "wooden O" goes beyond simply suggesting that the spectators observe the physical structure of the playhouse. Cognitively, this speech alters the parameters of what is called the "container schema" for the performance. A container schema is a mental construct that allows each of us to conceptualize something as existing "within" something else. The two critical components of this schema are the boundary of the "interior" and the articulation of a discrete object that is positioned within that interior space. This appears straightforward when we think about "a butterfly in a jar," but establishing a strict boundary for the interior becomes more difficult when we think about "a butterfly in the garden."[5]

Thus in verbally articulating the surrounding architecture of the theatre building itself, rather than, say, the stage edge, as the boundary of the "interior space," Shakespeare invokes a container schema that encompasses not only the stage action, but the activity of the spectators as well. Although the action of the play's narrative scenes allows the boundary of the performance space to recede back to the edges of the stage, the repeated stretching of the performative envelope by the Shakespearean Chorus between the formal acts allows the audience to become increasingly comfortable with their ability to shift the cognitive boundary of the performance space outward to include their own role within the production in a more conscious way. Thus when King Henry gets to a major "public" speech such as the famous St. Crispin's Day speech, which is ostensibly performed for the onstage audience of his soldiers, the audience would be more likely to recognize the metatheatrical implications of the moment and to include themselves more consciously as part of Henry's "band of brothers," particularly if the actor playing Henry were to lift his own eyeline above the heads of his onstage soldiers to include the spectators as well.

Of course, we have no evidence that indicates where the actor playing King Henry might cast his gaze in the original production, and we can do nothing more than make a reasoned argument as to what effect such a choice might have had on the play's spectators. But by examining how Shakespeare uses dramaturgical techniques to define his audience's conception of space we can better understand the potential options that practitioners have to work with in mounting future productions. *Henry V* stands as a prime example of how space can be shaped again and again within a single performance in ways that alter the perceptual/cognitive processes of the spectators.

A dramatist's use of spatial dramaturgy need not always be so meta-theatrically oriented. More narratively driven techniques are important as well. Cassandra's "vision" of the Furies who sit upon the roof of the House of Atreus in *The Oresteia* provides a useful example:

> These roofs—look up—there is a dancing troupe
> that never leaves ...
>   —The Furies!
> They cling to the house for life. They sing,
> sing of the frenzy that began it all,
> strain rising on strain, showering curses
> on the man who tramples on his brother's bed.
> (*Agamemnon:* 1189–1198)[6]

Translations naturally differ in their depiction of this scene, but all contain some variation of the direct exhortation from Cassandra to shift the chorus' (and the spectators') line of sight to the roofline of the palace.[7] The combination of the presence of the physical skene—posing as the palace for this production—Cassandra's exhortation to "look up—there," and what I have to assume was the reinforcing influence of the actor's own line of sight (possibly even a pointing finger) cognitively conjures the Furies into the physical space of the Theatre of Dionysus in what Andrew Sofer would describe as an instance of "dark matter." In Sofer's conception, dark matter becomes a kind of symbolic term used to describe unseen objects of theatrical relevance; Macbeth's dagger is the prototypical exemplar. Though utterly imaginary, instances of dark matter create a kind of "charged negative space" on the stage; they are objects that are both "not there" and "not not there."[8] In theatrically conjuring the dark-matter-Furies of Cassandra's vision, Aeschylus not only postulates the physical location of the Furies, but also encourages the audience's gaze to linger at the ridgeline of the skene as he animates their presence with dancing and singing.

This moment is an interesting example of spatial dramaturgy because it not only displays the playwright's ability to precisely control the gaze of the spectator, but it is also an example of how spectators can be "forced" to cognitively "misread" the physical objects that they can see within the stage space. As with most of the physical objects within a performance space, the skene in this scene has both a "real" identity (big chunk of physical scenery) as well as a "fictive" one (the palace of Agamemnon). Playwrights use a variety of techniques for imbuing physical scenery and props with their fictive identities, but in this instance the spectators' perception of the skene-as-palace is driven by the elementary spatial relations that support the cognitive conception of the Furies as being *on* something; the perception of the "House of Atreus" rather than the skene is cognitively implied within the perception of the invisible Furies.[9] Here the palace appears in the spectator's perception as a "situational anaphor," which is an entity whose presence is implied by a situation. Our ability to automatically insert situational anaphors into our perceptual processes is what allows dozens of tables, chairs, menus, and utensils to appear in our mind's eye when we read that a scene is taking place in a restaurant.[10] In many ways, this is simply a reinforcement of the skene-as-palace perception that is established in the opening moments of the play, but Cassandra's speech reinforces the metaphorical connection of the building to the generations of cyclical vengeance that the physical building played host to. Aeschylus uses Cassandra's lines to subtly reassert the fictive identity of the physical skene as the palace not only of Agamemnon, but of Atreus, Thyestes, Pelops, and Tantalus as well. This moment of spatial dramaturgy is markedly different from what we see in *Henry V*, but both examples demonstrate the power that playwrights can wield over our perception of the physical reality that surrounds us.

Civic Spaces

Aeschylus had little control over the performative space in which his plays appeared. The disputes over which scenic elements he may have had at his disposal are numerous, but they were certainly minimal.[11] Further compounding the playwright's lack of scenic control was the fact that the Theatre of Dionysus itself was enormous, probably designed more to the purposes of the fifty-performer dithyrambs than to the familial disputes of the House of Atreus. More than anything, the Theatre of Dionysus was a place of communal gathering, a "Civic Space" where the polis assembled for many reasons, only one of which was to watch a play.[12] Thus the material arrangement of the classical Theatre of Dionysus would likely have established an "architecture of perception" for the spectators that differs greatly from most theatres that are purpose-built with small theatrical performances as their primary raison d'être. Yet a careful examination of the spatial dramaturgy of *The Oresteia* reveals a series of plays that did not struggle against the architecture of perception that the Theatre of Dionysus presented; rather, these plays seem to have exploited the particular spatial characteristics of this famous space to great theatrical advantage.

Although the large, semi-circular stone auditorium exemplified by the Theatre at Epidaurus has become our default conception for what a Greek theatre would have looked like, a cursory survey of the roughly 200 Greek theatres that have been located to date demonstrates that the differences in their layout are as striking as their similarities. Greek orchestras could be either circular or rectilinear (more often the latter); altars could be located centrally or to the side of the main playing area; and the theatron could open not just to the eastern sunrise but to almost any point on the compass. That said, in all but a very few instances, the theatron—the seating area for the polis—was designed with a relatively steep rake in an arc-like arrangement that wrapped around three sides of the orchestra.[13]

There are obvious pragmatic benefits to this design: the steeply raked rows gave spectators an unobstructed view of the orchestra, and also allowed more seats to be located closer to the stage, thus improving acoustics. These pragmatic concerns aside, however, the theatron also organized the spectators spatially in a way that allowed them to easily see the faces of most of the other spectators. The ability to easily perceive the reactions of the rest of the members of the polis, as with a modern sports stadium, doubtless contributed a great deal of communitarian energy to the kind of events that these theatres were built to support.

Greek theatres were more than just sites of public entertainment; they were sites of civic gathering.[14] In such a space, the ultimate payoff for a play might easily arise from the socialized reaction of 15,000 spectators witnessing their fellow citizens respond to key moments of the play. A careful analysis of works like *The Oresteia* can reveal the ways that playwrights used the audience's ability to effortlessly observe one another's faces as a dramaturgical feature to be exploited, rather than as a problem to be overcome. An intriguing example can be observed in the scenic shift from Delphi to Athens in *The Eumenides*.

Internal shifts were relatively rare in the tragedies, but the completeness of the shift from Delphi to Athens is implied by the full exit from the stage of all the performers. How precisely the Temple of Athena was depicted is impossible to determine, but most scholars concede that the famous statue of Athena was somehow represented scenically; there is a clear reference by the Furies to Orestes clinging to the base of it.[15] The fact that the scene being set in the orchestra was a direct representation of the Temple of Athena, which stood only meters behind the spectators atop the Acropolis, must have sent waves of murmurs and amused looks of recognition through the audience. As with Shakespeare's reference to the "wooden O," the connection between the two statues would have altered the boundary of the container schema for the performance, stretching it to include not only the spectators, but the Acropolis as well. The impact of this moment would have been driven primarily by the spectators' experience of their communal response.

As in *Henry V*, the cognitive relocation of the audience of citizens to the interior of the space of performance is reinforced several other times throughout the remainder of *The Eumenides.* Just before the start of Orestes' formal trial, Athena leads out a chorus of ten jurors whom she refers to as "Men of Attica."[16] The configuration of this chorus was a clear reference to the ten demes that formed the political divisions within the Attic polis, and whose citizens were seated in tribal order in the semicircular theatron.[17] Far from being "too big," in this moment the Theatre of Dionysus suddenly becomes a rich concentration of the citizenry of hundreds of square kilometers condensed into a relative nutshell.

The fact that the trial ultimately ends in a hung jury might again have inspired observable reactions among the spectators in the theatron; all large communities find themselves faced with intractable internal divisions that easily sustain flocks of metaphorical Furies. In the play, the deadlock is ultimately broken by Athena herself, and the metaphorical connection between the goddess Athena and the Attic capitol that was her namesake seems clear: the leadership of Athens allowed the many divided tribes of the Attic region to rise above their petty divisions.

The architecture of perception imposed by the Theatre of Dionysus gave Aeschylus the opportunity to articulate these sorts of civically minded ideas using spatially driven methodologies. By referencing the actual presence of the demes in the auditorium in the form of the ten fictional onstage jurors, he encouraged his Attic citizen-spectators to shift their gaze from the stage to the auditorium and back again; in presenting his audience with a scenic replica of the nearby statue of Athena, Aeschylus again encouraged a perception of a space so large that the spectators would have been dislodged from their position as omniscient voyeurs, and reminded of their role as citizen-participants in a public festival. These ideas may or may not have been reinforced further via specific staging techniques; the connection between the jurors and the demes would have been made stronger, for example, if they were to stand at the outer edges of the central orchestra, directly in front of the demes in the auditorium. Aside from whatever references to staging remain in the lines of the plays themselves, the evidence for such specific staging is essentially nonexistent. Nevertheless, a careful analysis of the spatial dramaturgy of both the play and the space for which it was written can provide modern practitioners and critics with some creative insights as to how modern productions might be staged in order to at least partially replicate the experience of the original spectators.

The Eyeline of Orestes

Some parts of *The Oresteia* are less clear regarding the details of their spatial dramaturgy than others. But if we assume that Aeschylus actively used the civic space of the Theatre of Dionysus as a tool for constructing his polis-oriented plays, we can begin to make informed arguments as to how certain moments might have been staged.

One particularly important moment comes just before the end of *The Libation Bearers* when Orestes first lays eyes on the approaching Furies:

> No, no! Women—look—like Gorgons,
> shrouded in black, their heads wreathed,
> swarming serpents!
> —Cannot stay, I must move on ...
>
> No dreams, these torments,
> Not to me, they're clear, real—the hounds
> of mother's hate ...
>
> God Apollo!
> Here they come, thick and fast,
> their eyes dripping hate ...
>
> You can't see them
> I can, they drive me on! I must move on—
> (*The Libation Bearers*: 1047–1061)[18]

There are clear parallels here to Cassandra's visions in *Agamemnon*; Orestes' words conjure the Furies into spatial existence as approaching bodies of dark matter. But unlike Cassandra, Orestes fails to verbalize precisely from where the Furies are approaching. Some critics have described this moment as the onset of madness for poor Orestes, thus postulating that the Furies are not anywhere; after all, the Chorus cannot seem to see what so clearly terrifies Orestes.[19] But there is a problem with this idea because moments later the Furies appear, fully embodied as the primary choral figures in *The Eumenides*; either Orestes was not crazy, or now we all are.

So much of the meaning of this moment depends upon an element of the spatial dramaturgy that has been lost: where, precisely, did the actor playing Orestes *look* when he said these lines? One way or another, the eyeline of Orestes proves definitive here. Did he simply look offstage toward the same parados through which the Chorus/Furies would enter at the beginning to the next play? Did he look around wildly in every direction, swatting the air as if he were truly mad? Did he look off beyond the western edge of the theatre toward the hill and the Areopagus (the legendary dwelling place of the furies), which lay just beyond the Acropolis? Perhaps, even more evocatively, he looked over the heads of the chorus of Libation Bearers at the members of the polis itself. This last choice would establish yet another spatial connection between the quarrelsome Athenian tribal units and the Furies. As discussed above, connections of this kind would become increasingly prominent in *The Eumenides*, in which the Furies appear as the Chorus, the onstage representatives of the collective citizenry.

In the absence of evidence, conjecture remains our only option, but Aeschylus' consistent dramaturgical engagement with the civic space of his theatre gives some weight to the idea that the eyeline of Orestes might have located the Furies as both "not present" and "not not present" within the ranks of the spectators in the theatron itself. To end the second play of the trilogy with such a direct reference to the audience is a bold choice, and one that foreshadows the dramatic shift toward the metatheatrical that would become so much more prominent in *The Eumenides*. By directing his gaze at the spectators, the actor playing Orestes would have created a moment of narrative disturbance in which confused looks of "why is he looking at us" might have circulated among the spectators, powerfully stretching the boundary of the container schema for that performative moment to include the audience as the source of Orestes' fear. On its own, such a disruption of the usual narrative flow would be awkward and disruptive, but in the context of the full trilogy, it could serve as a powerful example of the playwright's control of the dramaturgical characteristics of the civic space in which he worked.

According to the Aristotelian standards that we continue to embrace, *The Oresteia* is a rather eccentric example of a tragedy. For one, the trilogy as a whole is not particularly tragic. Agamemnon, Cassandra, Clytemnestra, and Aegisthus all meet "premature" ends, but none of these characters ever really rise to the level of what we usually think of as a tragic hero. In fact, the entire question of whom the audience is meant to align their sympathies with is enormously complicated. The oft-repeated idea that "the one who acts must suffer" sums up the play's tendency to endear us to *all* those who have been wronged by the actions of others: we empathize with Clytemnestra's grief over the loss of her daughter Iphigenia, with Cassandra over the loss of her nation, and with Orestes and

Electra over the loss of their father. One can even feel a twinge of sympathy for the more prototypically unsympathetic Aegisthus; it must, indeed, be painful to grow up in exile knowing that your father ate your brothers. Yet our sympathies are always sharply curtailed by the actions that those characters subsequently take. The greatest strength of *The Oresteia* is, of course, its ability to humanize the senseless cycles of retribution that form the core of the play's narrative. Although from a strictly Aristotelian perspective the dramaturgy of *The Oresteia* appears flawed, from the perspective of the play's spatial dramaturgy, constructed to take advantage of the civic space of the Theatre of Dionysus, the trilogy operates quite effectively in its attempt to draw the inherently heterogeneous elements of the Attic polis toward a place of greater civic cohesion.

Notes

1. Oliver Taplin, *The Stagecraft of Aeschylus: The Dramatic Use of Entrances and Exits in Greek Tragedy* (London: Oxford University Press, 1977); David Wiles, *Tragedy in Athens: Performance Space & Theatrical Meaning* (New York: Cambridge University Press, 1997).

2. The specific phrase "architecture of perception" that I am employing here comes from an insight in Herbert Blau's book *The Audience*. As Blau states, "The distance of looking and the distance of listening . . . are determined largely by the material arrangement of theatre space, the architecture of perception." Herbert Blau, *The Audience* (Baltimore: Johns Hopkins University Press, 1990), 86. Although Blau's discussion operates in more general terms than mine, I think that his emphasis on the connection between the material arrangement of the theatrical space and the spectator's perception of the performance is useful, and I therefore employ the phrase "architecture of perception" often here in order to reference the connection between the structure of the physical space and the perception of the events that occur within it.

3. There is some doubt about whether the location of the original production was the Globe Theatre or the Curtain Theatre. For more on this see James Shapiro, *1599, A Year in the Life of William Shakespeare* (London: Faber, 2005), 99. For more details about the physical proximity of these theatres to physical sites of gambling and prostitution, see Andrew Gurr and John Orrell, *Rebuilding Shakespeare's Globe* (New York: Routledge, 1989), 53–59.

4. Jennifer M. Groh, *Making Space: How the Brain Knows Where Things Are* (Cambridge, Mass.: Harvard University Press, 2014), 69–83.

5. George Lakoff and Mark Johnson, *Philosophy in the Flesh: The Embodied Mind and Its Challenge to Western Thought* (New York: Basic Books, 1999), 30–32.

6. Aeschylus, "Agamemnon," in *The Oresteia*, trans. Robert Fagles (New York: Penguin Books, 1979), 150.

7. The original script, of course, had no stage directions; thus the only spatial cues that we have to work with are embedded in the lines themselves. Clifford Ashby, *Classical Greek Theatre: New Views of an Old Subject* (Iowa City: University of Iowa Press, 1999), 6; Taplin, *Stagecraft of Aeschylus,* 30–31.

8. Andrew Sofer, *Dark Matter: Invisibility in Drama, Theatre, and Performance* (Ann Arbor: University of Michigan Press, 2013), 3–9.

9. Lakoff and Johnson, *Philosophy in the Flesh,* 31.

10. William H. Levine and Celia M. Klin, "Tracking of Spatial Information in Narratives," *Memory & Cognition* 29, no. 2 (2001): 327.

11. Ashby, *Classical Greek Theatre,* 62–77.

12. Ibid., 78; Oddone Longo, "The Theatre of the Polis," in *Nothing to Do with Dionysos,* ed. John J. Winkler and Froma I. Zeitlin (Princeton, N.J.: Princeton University Press, 1990), 15–16.

13. Ashby, *Classical Greek Theatre,* 15–17, 24–37, 98–117.

14. Longo, "Theatre of the Polis," 13–16; John Camp and Elizabeth Fisher, *The World of the Ancient Greeks* (London: Thames & Hudson, 2002), 82, 134, 185.

15. Taplin, *Stagecraft of Aeschylus,* 375–77.

16. Aeschylus, *The Eumenides,* in *The Oresteia,* 262. Translations vary in their description of this group; Fagles actually uses the phrase "men of Greece"; Herbert Weir Smyth, E. H. Plumptre, and Gilbert Murray variously employ "Attica"; and Carl H. Mueller and E. D. A. Morshead reference "Athens" instead. But the reference in the original Greek is to "Attikos," which encompassed the entire city-state that extended throughout the Attic peninsula, rather than just the fortified urban center of Athens itself (Αθήνα), but it does not, by any means, extend to include the entirety of "Greece" (Ελλάς). Aeschylus is clearly referencing the region represented by the citizens of the polis assembled in the theatron.

17. Longo, "Theatre of the Polis," 16.

18. Aeschylus, *The Libation Bearers,* in *The Oresteia,* trans. Robert Fagles (New York: Penguin Books, 1979), 224–26.

19. Taplin, *Stagecraft of Aeschylus,* 359–60.

"It Told Us What To Do"

The Anthropomorphizing of Theatre Buildings in Contemporary Practice

Lisa Marie Bowler

An early morning in April 2012. The ornate circular space of Shakespeare's Globe Theatre feels slightly muted, its colors flattened by the grey London light. Bare and unlined with people, it also feels bigger than it does during evening and afternoon performance times. The group of actors I have just picked up from the hotel and accompanied here has recovered from the initial impact of entering the space; their first reaction was a dazed, or maybe awed, silence, which has now made way for exploratory action. Some, in tourist mode, are posing for pictures. Others have already climbed up onto the high platform stage— awkwardly, as the stage manager has not yet attached the wooden steps leading up to it—and are trying out movements or gestures, extending an arm, silently mouthing lines. They are adjusting their postures to the space, still hesitant, but already standing taller as they gaze outward into the empty vertical tiers of the wooden amphitheatre. I interpret their actions as an attempt to align themselves with the space, mirroring its shape and testing its reactions.

I am here as a researcher, but I am also part of the team of Globe staff and volunteers running the Globe to Globe Festival. Over a period of six weeks the festival brings thirty-seven international theatre companies to London to perform all of Shakespeare's thirty-seven plays, each in a different language. If this seems like an Olympian endeavor, it is: the festival is part of the 2012 Cultural Olympiad, the arts program accompanying the London Games.[1] The schedule is tight and each company has only one morning of stage rehearsal time before its first performance that same afternoon. A second performance will follow on the evening of the next day, by which time a new company will have already arrived and completed its morning rehearsals and matinee performance. This system ensures that every day of the festival sees two different productions in two different languages.

We are back onstage, and the Globe's resident "Master of Movement" arrives.[2] She welcomes each actor individually, asking which part they are playing, making them feel as if they had been born to do just this. Eventually the group coalesces into a circle on the stage. Everyone holds hands. I am told to join in and we close our eyes. She speaks: *Below you are boards made of 400-year-old oak. Above you, in the painted Heavens, is the fire of Jupiter. Feel yourself growing into the floor, receive the light from above. The architecture of this theatre supports your entire structure. It asks only one thing of you: that you come with an open heart.*[3] The ritual I am participating in is called "Introduction to the Stage." It gives the newly arrived actors the opportunity to spend their first hour of stage rehearsals in the company of an experienced Globe practitioner and to explore the space through a series of exercises. She continues: *The Globe is based on the proportions of your own body. If you stretch your arms out, the distance between your fingertips is the same length as your height. You form a perfect circle, like the Globe itself.*[4] We spread out onstage, stretch out our arms to the sides, and imagine a circle drawn around us, touching the top of our head, our fingertips, and our feet. *Turn slowly around your axis and feel how the circle becomes a sphere. This is your personal space.*[5] We walk around the stage in our spheres of personal space, taking care not to "dent" the others' spheres. *Can you feel the circle of the theatre embracing you? Trust it, it will tell you what to do.*[6]

"The theatre will tell you what to do." I begin with this account of my experience of rehearsals at the Globe because it illustrates some of the challenges that the topic of architectural anthropomorphism poses. On the one hand, the idea that the theatre building as a spatial structure is able to intervene in and direct performers' actions mirrors Henri Lefebvre's dictum that "space commands bodies, prescribing or proscribing gestures, routes and distances to be covered."[7] On the other, the leap from here to the image of a fully anthropomorphized theatre building—a communicative being able to embrace, to support, to disclose—is a large one. Yet it is a leap that is regularly made by theatre practitioners talking about their buildings, not just at the Globe. The Royal Shakespeare Company's executive director, Vikki Heywood, for example, has described the last performance on the old Royal Shakespeare Theatre's stage—a special "farewell event" before demolition crews moved in on it in 2007—in distinctly anthropomorphic terms: "We wanted a ceremony, a moment when we put the theatre to sleep. The company needed that."[8]

Peter Brook's Bouffes du Nord in Paris, too, has consistently been spoken and written about as if it were a real person. To name but a few instances: the actress Natasha Parry claims that "it has its likes and dislikes. I've seen it with certain outside productions when it sort of shrinks back into itself and becomes dismal and grey: it's tempting to say the theatre isn't happy."[9] Peter Brook himself calls the cracks in the building's walls its "wrinkles and pockmarks,"[10] and Jean-Claude Carrière (who adapted the *Mahabharata* for Brook's stage and film versions) describes their first visit to the derelict Bouffes du Nord as a magical Sleeping Beauty moment with the theatre as its protagonist: "There was a touch of the fairy tale about it—a space seemed to be waiting for us in a state of slumber, miraculously preserved from the demolitions of the 1970s which destroyed many sites in Paris. . . . The Bouffes was unimaginable for us: *it* told *us* what to do."[11] Again, in the same way as at the Globe, the building is posited as an expressive structure that enters into communication with the human beings who inhabit it.

Traditional architectural discourses on the ways in which buildings signify only partially address this phenomenon, because they generally focus on buildings' mimetic properties—how they can be read. Here, however, the question is slightly different. The theatres in the given examples are believed to not only represent something, but to also be able to *do* (i.e., embrace, sleep, shrink) and to *speak* (i.e., tell us what to do, or about their dislikes). What performers essentially describe when they use such imagery is their perception of being acted upon by the building or space: They feel somatically affected by it and choose (or are compelled) to articulate this sense of being affected in anthropomorphic terms. If they feel embraced by the space, the building must be doing the embracing. That such anthropomorphizing even seems to be necessary points to a lack of vocabulary to accurately describe our somatic responses to the constructed environment in general. The building-as-body analogy is a way of addressing this imbalance, as it substitutes the static architectural structure for a living, moving body, allowing for active verbs to be used in relation to it ("it protects," "it expects me to," "it draws me in," "it resonates," "it forbids"). As this is an essentially phenomenological approach, the anthropomorphizing of the theatre building requires a focus on how architecture is perceived rather than how it measures up in objective reality.

Perhaps because this sidelining (or bracketing) of objective reality feels odd for people unaccustomed to phenomenological thinking, the examples that I quoted earlier of theatre practitioners using the building-as-body analogy remain somewhat tentative. Reading the quotes in their larger contexts, it becomes clear that the idea of the theatre-as-body is rarely explored in much detail at all.[12] It is frequently alluded to as an evocative image, but instead of sustained engagement with the idea there usually follows a subtle shift toward discussions of the building's atmosphere or history. Indicative of the aforementioned lack of effective vocabulary to describe spatial experience, this reticence in developing the building-as-body analogy also appears to show a lack of conviction that a theatre's architecture should indeed be the cause of its perceptual, even emotional impact. It is much more common to ascribe this impact to a theatre's sense of history and tradition—to an implicit knowledge of a history that is closely connected to its architecture but not intrinsic to it. Specifically at the Globe, actors use the building-as-body analogy as if its cause were the sense that the theatre is alive with (or because of) the memory of Shakespeare. My aim in what follows is to disentangle these intertwined, sometimes blurred discourses. I ask how the body of the building comes to be marked by history, and whether such markings contribute to, or are indeed the cause of, the building's ability to act with agency.

I begin with the first part of this question: How does the "body" of a building come to be marked by history? The phenomenological approach of focusing on how the building is perceived allows us to say that it "stands," as a body would, bearing witness to events. The philosopher Richard Shusterman attributes this impression to the experiential primacy of the lived human body, which functions as a "gestural template" not just for architecture, but also for perception generally.[13] Developing this idea further, we can say that the building-as-body tells us about the events it witnesses by displaying markings, weathering, wear, and sedimentation of different kinds on its outer surface, its skin. "Time does not pass in architecture, it accumulates,"[14] writes David Leatherbarrow, an architectural theorist and phenomenologist who has analyzed the ways in which a building's surfaces can collect and harbor memories. He understands an expressive building to be one that absorbs and reveals traces of life, being shaped by use as much as it shapes patterns of action and behavior.

Exemplary of this process of materials taking on a sense of time passing is the work of the Swiss architect Peter Zumthor. By paying attention to how certain materials react to environmental factors and employing them accordingly, he anticipates that timber steps will become worn down in a particular way, floorboards will become uneven by use, metals will become patinated or polished through everyday handling, and glass or varnish will be dulled and marked by innumerable small scratches.[15] All of this is part of his design intention. As a result, his buildings seem to amplify their own aging processes. They continue to develop and evolve under the influence of various forces, which Zumthor, unlike many architects, regards not as forces of corruption but as a continuation of his design. The body of the building offers active resistance to the flows of life and is marked in the process.

This concept provides the first useful model for thinking about how a theatre—particularly an old theatre building—can be understood to be communicative: its markings (or injuries, if you will) trace past events, map flows of movement, and display patterns of use and behavior. Theatre buildings can thus be said to communicate their past in a language composed of creaking boards, dark stained wood, chipped plaster, polished gold, and fading velvet. Auratic markings, such as the roll call of names carved into or scribbled on a backstage wall, or a particular groove in the surface of an old stage indicating a preferred spot for actors to stand, are easy to understand and translate, but they are not, as this essay aims to show, the only ways in which theatre buildings communicate. On a deeper level, architectural spaces reflect social structures and hierarchies through their layout and design, in how they regulate the flow and behavior of people. Expressed in anthropomorphic terms, this means that buildings are able to *enforce* social and cultural conventions. Some West End theatres from the Victorian period, for example, still have separate entrances for the upper galleries, whose original function was to keep those who could only afford cheap seats out of the main foyers and well away from the upper classes in their finery. Feeling oneself being ushered through the winding passageways of such theatres' innards, the architecture's ability to direct (as well as entice, intimidate, or mislead), is palpable.

The theatre-as-body thus induces actions. As well as being acted upon and being marked in the process, it acts upon others. Historians and theatre practitioners have sought to use this insight, hoping that older forms of theatre and performance, as well as specific events, might be conserved in the active memory of spaces and buildings. Formulated by Lefebvre, the theory behind this hope involves an "animating principle," or presence, of an architectural body that "reproduces itself within those who use the space in question, within their lived experience."[16] This could be taken to mean that a given space will automatically elicit the same kinds of behavior from any group of people and that a building will tell us exactly and unequivocally how it should be used. The idea is particularly pertinent for the Globe Theatre and for Shakespearean performance traditions. Very few original traces remain of either, so the idea that knowledge of Shakespeare's stagecraft may be recovered by learning how to re-inhabit the historical space that produced it in the first place is a powerful one. The hope that Shakespearean performance traditions would "reproduce themselves" in the bodies of contemporary actors and audiences if only they inhabited the correct Elizabethan architecture was one of the main motivations behind the Globe reconstruction project.[17] The theatre as it stands today is regarded by many as a Shakespearean "personality," an actor as much as a keeper of memories. My introductory examples of the ritual and exercises I observed at the Globe provide a sense of this expectation.

But there are problems. It would be a misinterpretation of Lefebvre to assume that a space will exactly reproduce cultural practices and forms of behavior even when the times, society, and culture have changed completely.[18] The tendency of Globe practitioners to assume that because their theatre is as close as possible a replica of the original building, it somehow "knows" and can tell us about Shakespeare, has been sharply criticized by theatre scholars. Catherine Silverstone, for example, has drawn a direct connection between the anthropomorphic imagery used by Globe practitioners in relation to their building and its lack of historical authenticity. She argues that the sense of presence that the building-as-body exudes is the result of a psychological conjuring trick, motivated by a profound experience of absence that has pervaded the architectural reconstruction project from the beginning: absence of Shakespeare himself, of the original building, of authenticity. She asserts that the physical theatre building has come to be seen as an Ersatz-source of presence for many of those working there: "It seems a psychological necessity for those inhabiting the space to conceive of it in anthropomorphic terms. Motivated by a desire to reconstruct and invoke the absent Globe, and by extension Shakespeare, the project's participants are ultimately satiated by the sense of presence they crave (and even demand)."[19] I would not go that far. There is no question that the building is present and, through its architectural reality, exudes a sense of presence. Just because the Globe is not a witness able to authentically speak of Elizabethan times—as we have already established—does not mean that it cannot tell us about other things, and the danger of categorically dismissing any form of anthropomorphism is losing sight of those things that the building *can* tell us. Before offering an answer to what these things might be, I briefly turn to another example of anthropomorphized theatre buildings and their complicated relationship with history and memory.

While the Globe, as a replica that is barely twenty years old, lacks the sedimentations and markings that might otherwise have spoken about its history, the theatres most associated with Peter Brook are bodies heavily marked by the forces of time and decay. Explicitly described by him as "wrinkles and pockmarks," these markings and injuries have been carefully preserved and even sometimes exaggerated, to show how much the building has lived through.[20] Repeating a process first developed at the Bouffes du Nord, the Majestic Theater in Brooklyn, now BAM Harvey Theater, was discovered as a ruin in 1987 and renovated in such a way as to not lose the aesthetic of the ruin. A contemporary review in the *New York Times*, entitled "Restoring a Theater to Its Decrepit State," could not resist exaggerating the irony of this process: "Paint crumbles from walls. Fragments of friezes are chipped and mottled. Ducts are exposed. Decades of dirt encrust the proscenium. A rare plaster disease invades the ceiling. This is the 'new' Majestic Theater in downtown Brooklyn. Its restoration cost $5 million."[21] Another review, entitled "Putting Old Wrinkles into a Theater's New Face,"[22] picked up on Brook's anthropomorphizing of the theatre, equating its cracked wall with an aged face and even layering the image further, evoking the intensely theatrical trope of the actor with old-fashioned stage makeup of painted lines and wrinkles. The sense of history that was inscribed to the space here is not entirely false; it is, after all, a historical building. But it is also manufactured, belying, if nothing else, its recently renovated state. David Wiles writes that "it is a feature of successful performance spaces that a sense of the past is inscribed in the present,"[23] and this seems to justify a certain level of dissimulation. The same applies, for example, to the Old Vic Theatre in London, which was deliberately given a patina of history after its renovation. It is not enough for a building to have a history; audiences and practitioners prefer it to also *look* like it has a history.

So what do these markings of time, both contrived and real, do, and what is their relationship with the animate being of the theatre building? The haunting, almost morbid, quality of the conjuring of old age, physical injury, and disease that characterized the *New York Times* description of the Brooklyn Majestic suggests that its markings are read as ghostly signs of a dead past. Marvin Carlson has coined the term "ghosting" for the process whereby the theatrical aesthetic comes to include the experience of being haunted by layers of memories of texts, bodies, and spaces.[24] The idea of the ghost as the animating principle of the anthropomorphized theatre building, however, is paradoxical, as it assumes that the sense of presence felt by audiences and performers as they inhabit the building is due to an absence, a negative of presence—the ghost. An example describing such a haunting presence is offered by David Williams, who, writing about the Bouffes du Nord, compares the theatre's back wall to a "Turin shroud," an imprint of a long-dead face: "The towering back wall, over 50 feet high, is scarred and pitted by the wear and tear of the years, like an aged human face, but the only sign of the former stage and its machinery is a wide horizontal band traversing the wall and the dark square stain above, framing the old stage picture, like a Turin shroud for a dead form of theatre."[25] The anthropomorphized image of the theatre building and the idea of architectural suffering come together here in a powerful evocation of the theatre as an oracle of the past. And yet, as an explanation for the sense of presence, animation, and agency felt and described by theatre practitioners in relation to their theatre buildings, this interpretation of the animating principle as a "ghost" does not go far enough. It focuses too much on what is absent and not enough on what is materially present.

An alternative approach is offered by the anthropologist Tim Ingold and his discussion of animism, outlined in the book *Being Alive*.[26] He identifies a poverty of language in Western culture to accurately capture and describe how supposedly static, inanimate objects (including buildings) act on us—as perceptually they undoubtedly do. He argues that animistic cultures are more advanced in this sense, conceiving of objects as "hives of activity."[27] A building's agency and sense of animacy is not the result of an external ghost or spirit that is somehow magically added to it, but is already intrinsic to it, rooted in its composition and materiality: "Bringing things to life, then, is a matter not of adding to them a sprinkling of agency but of restoring them to the generative fluxes of the world of materials in which they came into being and continue to subsist."[28] The key word here is "materials": objects are understood not as stable entities but to be "pulsing with the flows of materials that keep them alive."[29] Ingold argues that it is by attending to an object's materiality that we can understand its agency: how it interacts with us and the world. Materials degrade, vibrate, oxidize, shrink—they *move*. For buildings this means that their active bodies are a combination of materials and form; in other words, their architecture. We saw how the architect Zumthor highlights the yielding, shifting quality of his materials and how the architectural bodies of theatres can draw us in, amplify, resonate, hide, or reveal. But this kind of engagement with buildings as active forms remains underdeveloped and poorly articulated, as the lack of confidence in the image of the anthropomorphized theatre building shows.

Even though we as theatre scholars talk about "materiality" and have been conscious, since theatre studies' emancipation from literature in the early twentieth century, of the importance of analyzing the material reality of the art form, we still do not define theatrical materials in any great detail. What, for example, are the properties and components of dust? How does oak resonate with the human voice compared to plaster or concrete, and why? What is the materiality of a spotlight—what is it made of, how does it behave? And how do dust and spotlight interact when they meet onstage?

My interpretation of the anthropomorphizing of theatre buildings by practitioners (and sometimes audiences) is that it is a first step toward answering such questions, because as an image it requires us to think of the building as a body being capable of concrete actions. What is more, it prompts us to go into much more detail in equating the building's architectural and material elements with bodily parts and their functions—the stage as the heart, for example, and its entrances and exits as systole and diastole, pumping the life blood of its actors through it.[30] The analogy's main potential lies in how it directs attention to what architecture *does*. However, as I have demonstrated, there is still a general tendency to attribute a theatre's sense of animacy to what it *knows*: to memories and ghosts of the past haunting its structures. Buildings are acted upon and marked by the forces of time, and these markings are often read as the reason for their expressiveness. But in fact it is the architecture itself—its material reality, form, and character—that makes theatre buildings able to "tell us what to do."

Notes

1. The Globe to Globe Festival took place from April 21 to June 9, 2012. It was part of the World Shakespeare Festival, which in turn was part of the 2012 Cultural Olympiad. Its resident academics were Susan Bennett and Christie Carson, who have since edited a book with reviews of all the performances in the festival from a variety of theoretical angles. Susan Bennett and Christie Carson, eds., *Shakespeare beyond English: A Global Experiment* (Cambridge: Cambridge University Press, 2013).

2. This is Glynn MacDonald, teacher of Alexander Technique, movement, and voice at the Globe since its opening in 1995.

3. Here and in the following (notes 3–6) I quote from my notes, which cover all the "Introduction to the Stage" rituals I attended during the festival. While the exact words used varied from day to day depending on factors such as the nature of the play, the responsiveness of the group or director, or whether a translator needed to be present, the references to circles, bodily proportions, and the "personality" of the Globe were a constant.

4. Ibid.

5. Ibid.

6. Ibid.

7. Henri Lefebvre, *The Production of Space* (Cambridge, Mass.: Blackwell, 1991), 143.

8. Vikki Heywood, interviewed in David Ward, *Transformation: Shakespeare's New Theatre* (Stratford-upon-Avon: RSC Enterprise, 2011), 4. In a three-year transformation process, the theatre was essentially gutted and rebuilt as a thrust stage, retaining most of the building's landmarked outer shell of 1932.

9. Natasha Parry, interviewed in Andrew Todd and Jean-Guy Lecat, *The Open Circle: The Theater Environment of Peter Brook* (New York: Palgrave Macmillan, 2003), 31.

10. Peter Brook describes Bouffes Du Nord: "The fact that it was materially

wounded, with wrinkles, pock marks and signs of having passed through life," in a lecture given to a symposium on performance space at Royal Holloway, University of London, September 1999, quoted in David Wiles, *A Short History of Western Performance Space* (Cambridge: Cambridge University Press, 2003), 263.

11. Todd and Lecat, *Open Circle*, 9.

12. As the introductory examples show, the image of the anthropomorphized theatre building is predominantly used by performers and practitioners. Theatre scholars, including for example David Wiles and Catherine Silverstone, have on occasion commented on such anthropomorphizing, but there currently exists no in-depth study of the phenomenon.

13. Richard Shusterman, "*Somaesthetics and Architecture: A Critical Option*," presentation at the International Bauhaus Colloquium, Weimar, April 1–5, 2009, webcast, 17:20. Accessed November 20, 2014, https://www.youtube.com/watch?v=49xX6piR6gM.

14. David Leatherbarrow, *Architecture Oriented Otherwise* (New York: Princeton Architectural Press, 2009), 82.

15. Peter Zumthor, *Thinking Architecture* (Basel: Birkhäuser Verlag, 2010), 24.

16. Lefebvre, *Production of Space*, 137.

17. See for example Andrew Gurr's essay "Shakespeare's Globe: A History of Reconstruction and Some Reasons for Trying," in *Shakespeare's Globe Rebuilt*, ed. J. R. Mulryne and Margaret Shewring (Cambridge: Cambridge University Press, 1997).

18. To give an example: when I visit one of the Victorian theatres mentioned earlier in the essay, I am not compelled by its spatial organization to reenact the divisions and hierarchies of Victorian society, even though it retains separate entrances and passageways for the different tiers.

19. Catherine Silverstone, "Shakespeare Live: Reproducing Shakespeare at the 'New' Globe Theatre," *Textual Practice* 19, no. 1 (2005): 33–34, doi:10.1080/0950236042000329636.

20. Wiles, *Short History*, 263. The contrast between the Globe and Brook's theatres is striking: the new Globe looks pristine, with no attempts having ever been made to make it look older than it is. It will of course, with time, acquire markings, but they will speak of its twenty-first century history and be very different from those on an original Elizabethan building.

21. Susan Heller Anderson, "Restoring a Theater to Its Decrepit State," *New York Times*, October 13, 1987.

22. Michael Kimmelman, "Putting Old Wrinkles into a Theater's New Face," *New York Times*, October 25, 1987.

23. Wiles, *Short History*, 59–60.

24. He calls the theatre building "one of the most haunted of human cultural structures." Marvin Carlson, *The Haunted Stage: The Theatre as Memory Machine* (Ann Arbor: University of Michigan Press, 2001), 132.

25. David Williams, "'A Place Marked by Life': Brook at the Bouffes du Nord," *New Theatre Quarterly* 1, no. 1 (1985): 40, doi:10.1017/S0266464X0000141X.

26. Tim Ingold, *Being Alive: Essays on Movement, Knowledge and Description* (London: Routledge, 2011).

27. Ibid., 29.

28. Ibid.

29. Ibid.

30. The image of the Globe stage as a pumping heart comes from David Bradley: "The doors are thus the systole and diastole of the great heart-beat of the Elizabethan stage as it fills and empties, fills and empties." David Bradley, *From Text to Performance in the Elizabethan Theatre* (Cambridge: Cambridge University Press, 1992), 29.

Wartime Collaboration

Theatrical Space and Power in Conquered Los Angeles

Andrew Gibb

In April and May of 1855, a San Francisco weekly, *The Golden Era*, printed a three-part serial entitled "The Drama on the Pacific: First Theatricals in California," providing future theatre scholars with the first published history of theatre in the Golden State.[1] That journalistic chronicle contains a description of the first recorded theatrical production in what is now the city of Los Angeles: a series of performances mounted during the occupation of that city by US soldiers near the end of the US-Mexico War of 1846–48.[2] For the theatre historian, J. E. Lawrence's account is maddeningly uneven—by turns painstaking and imprecise, chauvinistic and culturally aware, and frequently contradictory. But if the text is closely read through the context of subsequent scholarship on nineteenth-century *Californio* (Mexican Californian) society, a remarkable tale emerges from the confusion: one of power, class, resistance, and collaboration (in both the theatrical and wartime senses). Bringing this story to light requires challenging the assumptions about theatrical space that lie at the heart of Lawrence's account. That this should prove necessary serves as a reminder to theatre historians that spaces of performance are not only a reflection of how a given culture defines performance, but also of how it perceives power.

Lawrence's serialized history begins with the assertion that "theatrical representation in California commenced with the first unfurling of the American Flag on the Western border of our Continent," a statement revealing an unabashed Anglo-centric bias. And yet, Lawrence's nationalist fervor led the author to extensively document the theatrical activities of the US soldiers who came to California during the US-Mexico War, inadvertently contributing to the history of theatre in Los Angeles.[3]

In the second installment, Lawrence tells of an entire theatrical season offered in Los Angeles by the soldier-actors of a unit known as the New York Volunteers, beginning in June of 1848 and lasting until September of that year. In a three-hundred-seat theatre apparently built for the occasion, the Volunteers gave performances of *The Golden Farmer*, *The Idiot Witness*, *Bombastes Furioso*, and "several more dramas and farces," together with *The Marble Statue* and "other pantomimes." Lawrence goes on to identify eleven "members of the Thespian corps" by name, and details the warm reception the Volunteers received from the populace of occupied Los Angeles.[4] Given Lawrence's patriotic tone, these details paint a picture of industrious and talented New York boys, sharing the theatrical blessings of liberty with the art-starved inhabitants of "a distant and almost unknown dependency of a semi-barbarous Mexico," and in so doing winning the hearts and minds of the locals.[5]

In the very next installment of the history, however, appearing only two weeks later, this tale of Los Angeles theatrical genesis is revised. Lawrence admits to "performances in Spanish which preceded the advent of the Volunteers," productions that "alternated" with those of the Volunteers, once they arrived. These plays were apparently mounted in a theatre that "cost between five and six thousand dollars," a structure financed by "a gentleman from Mexico."[6] In order to incorporate this new information, the narrative must expand from a tale of magnanimous victors proffering the gift of art to a story of a bicultural rotating repertoire, or maybe even a multicultural theatre district.

In either of those scenarios, the story of the first theatrical performance in Los Angeles appears to demonstrate the power of art as an intercultural bridge, even when the cultures in question are separated by the great gulf of war. Theatre may indeed have that power, and a bridging of Anglo American and Mexican Californian cultures may well have been at work with these productions. However, the contradictions apparent in Lawrence's two accounts, particularly as they involve the performance space, suggest that the shows reflected a more ambiguous reality: one of the powerful forces engaged in the complex intercultural negotiation of California's future. In short, the performances spatially represented a microcosm of events playing out beyond the theatre's walls.

Precisely locating these wartime productions requires a careful dissection of Lawrence's multiple accounts. In the first rendering of the events, the chronicler provides a good deal of information about the space: "In the month of June, 1848, a theatre was erected at Los Angeles. The stage was covered, and provided with a proscenium, drop curtain, and a tolerable supply of scenery. The auditorium was surrounded with adobe walls, and its occupants had only the heaven for their canopy. For choice seats, to be occupied by ladies and officers, there were balconies extending from the house, and the servants of the Spanish senoras [*sic*] brought chairs to be occupied by the latser [*sic*], who frequently graced the dress circle in considerable numbers. The whole place was fitted up to accommodate about three hundred persons."[7] At first glance, this seems to be a description of a typical Euro-American metropolitan theatre, complete with proscenium arch, balconies, and a dress circle. And yet, certain elements refuse to fit easily within that established architectural model for theatre spaces. Among them is the mention of adobe walls. Adobe was a common building material of Mexican California, but its manufacture and use was unfamiliar to the New Yorkers Lawrence seems to be crediting with the construction. Similarly, the lack of a roof would have set the theatre apart from contemporaneous New York theatres (or Mexico City ones, for that matter).[8]

Lawrence's second description of this (or some other) Los Angeles theatre, the one that appeared in the later May 13 issue, does little to explain the odd mixture of architectures suggested by the earlier account: "The Volunteers . . . opened the new theatre in the house of Don Antonio Coronel, on the 4th of July, 1848. Before this event, a gentleman from Mexico had, with the aid of several citizens of Los Angeles, constructed a theatre in which representations were given by a company of amateurs, Mexicans and native Californians, which were alternated in the latter part of 1848 with the performances by the N.Y. Volunteers. This theatre cost between five and six thousand dollars." [9] The first question raised by these two accounts is this: just how many theatres are being described? If the answer is two, then why did the soldiers not use the preexisting space for their shows? The next oddity is Lawrence's revised statement that the Volunteers' "new theatre," which he had earlier credited them with erecting, was apparently located "in the house of Don Antonio Coronel."

The most likely resolution of Lawrence's conflicting accounts is that they both refer to a single playing space. This possibility is supported by both an absence and a presence in the wider historical record of the period. As intriguing as is Lawrence's mention of a "five or six thousand dollar" theatre built by local elites, the existence of such a space in 1848 Los Angeles is extremely unlikely. The population of California before US conquest (estimated at 18,000) was not sufficiently large or concentrated enough to support a commercial theatre industry.[10] Dedicated spaces built to support such an industry were unknown to the region. If such a structure had been erected in Los Angeles in 1848 or before, its rarity would certainly have received the attention of contemporaries. The deafening silence of the historical record prior to 1848 seems to discredit Lawrence's account.

By contrast, the "house of Don Antonio Coronel" was a well-documented structure. Antonio Coronel, future mayor of Los Angeles, would have been the perfect host for the Volunteers. Among his many artistic interests, he was a devoted collector of plays.[11] Nevertheless, in the summer of 1848, Antonio could not have built a theatre within his own house for two simple reasons. First, he was away at the mines in Northern California, where many of his fellow *angelenos* had gone after gold was discovered in January of that year.[12] Second, even when in Los Angeles, Antonio did not have a house to do with as he wished; the as-yet-unmarried man still lived with his father, Ygnácio. The elder Coronel brought his family from Mexico to California in 1834. He worked temporarily for the local government and finally settled in Los Angeles in 1837. There he ran a small store and acted as the pueblo's schoolmaster, later serving in city government and becoming a local landowner.[13] For his growing family, Ygnácio built a large adobe townhouse at the corner of *Calle de los Negros* and *Calle del Aliso* in Los Angeles, a block from the plaza. This is clearly the structure Lawrence references, for in June of 1848, it was the only house Antonio Coronel could call home.

When Lawrence belatedly places the Volunteers' performances within the Coronel house, the seeming oddity of the Anglo American soldiers' choice of building materials is explained: the adobe walls that surrounded the audience were obviously those of Ygnácio Coronel's house. The theatre's lack of a roof is similarly demystified. The Coronels' home was a typical example of elite household construction in Mexican California. Although the ubiquitous adobe building material provided exceptional stability in an earthquake-prone region, it was not well suited to the construction of large, roofed interior spaces or multiple stories. When wealthy landowners sought to express their social position through space, their only option was to build outward. The layouts of elite *Californio* townhouses were characterized by long, narrow wings delineating a central courtyard. Although the interior rooms of such houses were not expansive, the footprints of the structures could be—and usually were—expanded by the addition of covered verandas extending beyond the exterior and/or interior walls. A photograph of the decaying Coronel house taken in the 1870s clearly indicates such exterior porches.[14]

When the floorplan of the Coronel adobe is superimposed upon Lawrence's initial account of the soldiers' playing space, the incongruity of an elaborate three-hundred-seat proscenium arch theatre in frontier Los Angeles is resolved. Lawrence, it would seem, borrowed the architectural terminology of contemporary metropolitan theatre spaces for use in depicting the Coronel house performances, possibly in an attempt to better characterize the theatrical activity of the soldier-performers as a civilizing act. Lawrence's description of "balconies extending from the house" for the use of "ladies and officers" who have their servants save seats for them recalls the boxes found in the theatres of Europe and the eastern United States, as does the author's characterization of these seating areas as "the dress circle."[15] Given our knowledge of the Coronel house, however, these "balconies" were almost certainly interior porches, no more than a few feet off the ground. Lawrence's choice of words must therefore be read as a cultural translation—one most likely aimed at appropriating the performances staged at this Mexican house for use in an Anglo American cultural history.

A similar act of translation can be seen in the author's recording of the theatre's audience capacity. For readers accustomed to the metropolitan theatres of 1855, a crowd of "about three hundred persons" was likely to be visualized within a theatre of three hundred seats, a structure requiring significant floorspace even given the small chairs and benches of nineteenth century theatres.[16] If, however, most of those audience members were standing in the courtyard of a home such as Coronel's, they would have taken up significantly less room.

Given the limitations on interior space characteristic of buildings like the Coronel adobe, any theatre on the premises must have been constructed fairground-style in the courtyard adjoining the house's wings. Lawrence's note that "the stage was covered" indicates such a detached structure. That such a temporary stage was "provided with a proscenium, drop curtain, and a tolerable supply of scenery" suggests considerable industry on the part of the builders.[17] As was the case with the so-called "balconies," Lawrence's vocabulary transforms the prosaic realities of spatially limited frontier staging into heroic acts of theatrical evangelization: by seemingly erecting a metropolitan-style theatre in 1848 Los Angeles, the New York soldier-actors brought the artistic benefits of their superior East Coast culture to a woefully uncivilized corner of the world.

But placing the Volunteers' performances in the house of Ygnácio Coronel, on a stage that may or may not have been built by them, complicates the picture of Anglo ingenuity and magnanimity that Lawrence paints. In fact, it suggests an altogether different interpretation, one that aligns the soldiers' plays with the theatrical production practices of Mexican California. Though Mexican California was connected to world markets through the export of its agricultural products, the penetration of capitalist forms of social exchange into local society was limited. Hard currency, for instance, was scarce. Large-scale economic exchanges were handled through an elaborate system of credit; smaller and more personal interchange happened through traditional gift-exchange structures of social mediation.[18] This largely moneyless economy offered little to attract touring theatre artists from either Mexico or the United States, even if audiences might be interested or if dedicated theatre spaces had existed to house them.

This is not to say that Mexican California had no experience of theatre. Antonio Coronel's love for the art attests to that, as do recorded productions going back as early as 1789, when the play *Astucias por heredar un sobrino a su tío* was mounted in Monterey.[19] But the mode of theatrical production and consumption in Mexican California was markedly different than that of large metropolitan centers, so much so that the blindness of a chronicler like Lawrence to *Californio* theatre may be attributed not only to national bias, but also perhaps to a failure to recognize local performance as theatre.

In the brief three decades between Mexican Independence in 1821 and US statehood in 1850, California transitioned from a colonial outpost economically dependent upon a string of Catholic missions to a semi-autonomous frontier society—made viable through trade with English, US, and Russian firms—and ruled by an oligarchy whose monopolization of agricultural land placed them at the center of local life. Decades of Spanish mercantilism had ensured that agriculture (specifically cattle ranching) was the only industry of significance, which meant that *Californio* ranchers were often the only ones offering a living to California laborers.[20] At the same time, however, the remoteness of California from other population centers meant that the limited labor force of California could not easily be replaced. As a result, the new oligarchs that divided California's ranchlands amongst themselves following Mexican independence were far more reliant upon their workers than were the capitalists of the European and American industrial revolutions. The Mexican Californian economy was thus shaped by a mutual dependency that dictated a social structure that has been termed "seigneurial culture."[21] Within such a system, relationships between workers and ranchers were regulated primarily through close interpersonal exchanges dictated by mutually agreed upon expectations and properly performed behaviors. For landowners, these obligations included occasional acts of largesse, ranging from individual gifts to large communal celebrations. Fiestas involving feasting and dancing were common seigneurial offerings.

The production of theatre found its place in Mexican Californian society as just such a symbolically performed act of oligarchic benevolence. Though plays were infrequent events in the years before US conquest, when they were offered they were always mounted in the homes of elite *Californios*, and admission was never charged. Theatre was not a commercial venture; rather, it was a gift of local oligarchs to their dependents. Workers considered such entertainments to be their due, elites thought of them as patriarchal generosity but also obligation, and all understood them to be links that helped keep society in seigneurial balance.

An instructive parallel to the Mexican Californian experience, at least in terms of spatial arrangements, might be taken from the staging practices of Renaissance Europe. In his history of Western theatrical space, *Places of Performance*, Marvin Carlson details the development of court and private theatres, a phenomenon that began in Renaissance Italy and continued through the nineteenth century. Carlson traces the private theatres of the European nobility and bourgeois elite back to the ducal great halls of the Italian Renaissance, in which "performance space and audience space were now completely absorbed into the body of the palace and could be reached only by penetrating that space."[22] Carlson directly links the development of the ducal theatres to the earlier utilization of cortiles, public squares incorporated into the ducal palaces by surrounding them with a ring of official structures, leaving the center open to the sky. For Carlson, the prime example of such architectural and theatrical innovation is the enclosing of such a cortile by the Duke of Ferrara in the fifteenth century, and his subsequent staging of performances within the newly created, semi-public space. Carlson relates how, beginning with the second of those performances, staged in 1487, "the duchess and other aristocratic ladies did not enter the cortile at all, but remained in a more private space, the loggia to the west of the cortile, above and behind the more general audience space."[23] From the enclosed, roofless playing space to the prescribed seating areas for elite women, the physical similarities between the entertainments offered by the Duke of Ferrara within his cortile and the productions at the Coronel adobe are striking. Of far greater interest, however, is the light that the Renaissance example sheds on the spatial expression of power represented by the 1848 Los Angeles shows.

Within the context of local *Californio* patterns of theatrical production, the spatial placement of the New York Volunteers' performances in the house of Ygnácio Coronel suggests a far more complex relationship between actors and audience than Lawrence takes into account. What may at first glance be seen as simple acts of diplomatic cultural exchange are transformed into contestations of sovereignty between conquered Mexican elites and the occupying US authority. In such negotiations, the Volunteers always retained the ultimate trump card of military force. Coronel, as a representative of the *Californio* ruling class, needed as much leverage as he could muster, and by hosting the performances within the bounds of his private property, he gained some of that needed leverage. In this manner, Coronel's courtyard functioned similarly to the ducal great hall, as "an unmistakable element of the prince's own spatial domain, the performance his possession, and the audience his guests."[24] In Coronel's case, not only were the audience members his guests, but the soldier-actors were as well.

Of course, the relationship between Coronel and the performers was obviously very different from the one between the Duke of Ferrara and the players he enlisted to perform in the ducal cortile. Within the power structure of occupied Los Angeles, even the lowest ranking of the US soldier-actors enjoyed some measure of authority over the wealthiest of *Californios*. But by drawing the occupiers into his "spatial domain," Coronel wrested back some measure of control over the political and social negotiations taking place outside his walls. By opening his house to the performances, Coronel made certain that the production of theatre in Los Angeles society remained firmly within the established *Californio* system of social exchange. The Spanish-language performances that he facilitated only further reinforced that arrangement. Through a production partnership with the conquerors, Coronel and his fellow *Californios* maintained their oligarchic status in the local political arena.

Evidence that the Volunteer shows functioned within a traditional *Californio* mode of theatrical production can be found within Lawrence's account. The description of an elite audience seating area—the porches figured as "balconies"—reveals more than an Anglo author's desire to translate local *Californio* architecture into a metropolitan theatrical idiom. At elite household entertainments in Mexican California, social hierarchy was always delineated spatially: the closer one was situated to the house, the higher one's rank. When feasting was involved, the owner and elite *Californio* guests dined in the large central room of the house, the *sala*, while laborers took the meals provided them standing or sitting in the courtyard of the house. Similarly, if and when dancing began, dependent workers would begin the festivities in the courtyard. At some point later in the evening the doors of the house would open, and the master and mistress would emerge with their elite entourage to claim the center of the courtyard as their stage, where they performed the highbrow dances that marked them as cultured, such as the very much in vogue waltz.[25]

Given the complex social meanings of theatrical production in Mexican California, the observations provided by Lawrence require a more nuanced reading. The porches of the Coronel adobe were not being used simply because they provided a better view of the action. The seating area of the "Spanish señoras" was the part of the makeshift theatre auditorium closest to the interior of the Coronel house. By claiming this privileged penumbra, the oligarchs of Los Angeles not only better enjoyed the show, but they also spatially performed their close personal connection to

Coronel, the local elite under whose aegis the shows were gifted to the community. The presence of the "officers" (one assumes US) in these same seats must also be read within the context of Californio seigneurialism. While the leaders of the occupation may have thought of their prominent seating as a sign of their own de facto ownership of the performances, *Californios* would have likely seen the sharing of the privileged space as an invitation extended to US elites to share in the existing power structure.

Another sign that *Californio* production modes held sway at the Volunteers' shows is Lawrence's silence on the subject of admission. Throughout the serialized history, Lawrence assiduously records the pricing of each and every soldier performance given during the occupation. Such data no doubt put a stamp of professionalism on all of the martial playmaking. But Lawrence provides no such information regarding admission fees in Los Angeles. The performances of the New York Volunteers were apparently offered free of charge. This was not an acting company renting a space for a short-term run; rather, Don Ygnácio Coronel, following the production traditions of prewar California, had invited the actors into his own home to perform for the pleasure of himself and his guests.

The interplay of space, power, and repertoire also suggests an interpretation of the Volunteers' theatricals in the Coronel home as a wartime negotiation. In the April 29 issue of the *Golden Era*, Lawrence lists the Volunteers' fare in detail, singling out *Bombastes Furioso* as one of the "favorites of the season."[26] William Barnes Rhodes' 1810 play, subtitled "A Burlesque Tragic Opera," is a send-up of the romantic tragedies popular on US and European stages in the early nineteenth century. Coincident to the present analysis, one of the likely literary sources *Bombastes* plays upon is the epic poem *Orlando Furioso*, penned by Ludovico Ariosto and dedicated to his sponsor, the Duke of Ferrara.[27] The play is a satire on military posturing, centered on its title character, a Miles Gloriosus type.[28] Although the satire is accomplished through the characterization of Bombastes as, indeed, bombastic, Rhodes does not confine his lampooning of martial pretense to the preposterous general. In the play's first scene, Bombastes enters at the head of his troops. The stage directions indicate that this army is to consist of "one Drummer, one Fifer, and two Soldiers, all very materially differing in size," the drastically uneven heights of the soldiers immediately marking them as objects of ridicule.[29] In the final moments of the play, nearly all of the main characters lie dead, victims of each other's vanity and stupidity. They then all miraculously arise, assuring the audience that "if some folks please, We'll die again to-morrow."[30] Such a play hardly seems calculated to inspire awe of military power.

Not only did the Volunteers play *Bombastes* multiple times over their four-month run, but Lawrence records that they chose it for the final performance marking the disbandment of the regiment in September of 1848. The playing of this piece by the Volunteers no doubt resonated variously across a spectrum of power differentials. The comic portrayal of Bombastes, for instance, gave the US soldiers a chance to laugh at their officers in public. The popularity of the piece among locals must have arisen, at least in part, from the spectacle of the conquering US soldiers sending up their own dominance. But all of this master-servant role reversal, so characteristic of the ancient comic texts from which Rhodes' script borrowed, ultimately served a more serious diplomatic function. To the "balconies" packed with *Californio* elites and their invited US officer guests, *Bombastes* would have played as a peace offering—an assurance to *Californios* that the future of California would not be determined by the might of US arms, but through the new oligarchic connections blossoming within the "dress circle."

Reading against the grain of Lawrence's text, and paying particular attention to space and the power relationships of performance, one can see the shows of the New York Volunteers and their *Californio* collaborators as an artistic and spatial representation of the intercultural negotiations that characterized the early years of US California. Through such power plays, theatrical and otherwise, Coronel and his fellow *Californio* elites were able to maintain their social position for the next twenty years. But beginning in the 1870s, a combination of economic factors and rising racial tensions led to the rapid decline of Mexican American influence in Southern California. What followed were decades of racial violence and segregation, including the development of separate and unequal English- and Spanish-language theatrical industries. Yet there is reason to hope that the Los Angeles theatre scene may finally be living up to its early intercultural potential. In October of 2014, the City of Los Angeles sponsored an unprecedented month-long celebration of Latina/o theatre, Encuentro 2014.[31] For the first time in the modern era, local civic leaders chose to celebrate and promote their city by highlighting theatre created by Latinas/os. Significantly, the site of that event, the Los Angeles Theatre Center, is located just a few short blocks from where the Coronel adobe once stood.

Notes

1. J. E. Lawrence, "The Drama on the Pacific: First Theatricals in California, Number 1," *The Golden Era*, April 15, 1855; "Number 2," April 29; "Number 3,"

May 13. George MacMinn relied upon Lawrence's labor in completing his *The Theater of the Golden Era in California* (Caldwell, Id.: Caxton Printers, 1941), which to date remains the most complete treatment of California theatre history. The author would like to thank the scholars of the 2015 SETC Theatre Symposium for their help in shaping this article, and Dr. Mark Charney, chair of the Texas Tech University Department of Theatre and Dance, for his critical role in supporting it.

2. The United States declared war on Mexico on May 13, 1846. US forces took Los Angeles on August 13 without a shot fired, but the poor diplomacy of the officer left in charge, Lieutenant Archibald Gillespie, soon led to an uprising. Los Angeles was retaken by US forces on January 9, 1847. When the New York Volunteers arrived in California a few months later, they were posted to Los Angeles. By the time they opened their shows, the city had been living under occupation for a year and a half. See Lizbeth Haas, "War in California, 1846–1848," in *Contested Eden: California before the Gold Rush*, ed. Ramón Gutiérrez and Richard J. Orsi (Berkeley: University of California Press, 1998), 333, 342–44.

3. "The Drama on the Pacific: First Theatricals in California, Number 1," *The Golden Era*, April 15, 1855.

4. "The Drama on the Pacific: First Theatricals in California, Number 2," *The Golden Era*, April 29, 1855. Lawrence's listing of the Volunteers' repertory reveals a mixture of melodrama, comedy, and farce common to the New York stage of the mid-nineteenth century. The reception of this eastern fare in its new surroundings is a subject I take up later in this essay.

5. "The Drama on the Pacific . . . Number 1," April 15, 1855.

6. "The Drama on the Pacific . . . Number 3," May 13, 1855.

7. "The Drama on the Pacific . . . Number 2," April 29, 1855.

8. Although the first professional theatre spaces in the Americas were open-air *corrales*, by the nineteenth century such structures were as unfamiliar to Mexicans as Shakespeare's Globe was to Victorian Londoners. Willis Knapp Jones, *Behind Spanish American Footlights* (Austin: University of Texas Press, 1966), esp. chapter 31.

9. "The Drama on the Pacific . . . Number 3", May 13, 1855.

10. This figure only takes into account Mexicans and Natives living in the settlements and ranchos of coastal California. The census of 1850 estimated the total Native population of the state to be 100,000. See Kevin Starr, *Americans and the California Dream: 1850–1915* (New York: Oxford University Press, 1974), 49; Miroslava Chávez-García, *Negotiating Conquest: Gender and Power in California, 1770s to 1880s* (Tucson: University of Arizona Press, 2004), 154.

11. Coronel's love of the theatre is documented in Nicolás Kanellos' *A History of Hispanic Theatre in the United States: Origins to 1940* (Austin: University of Texas Press, 1990), 11–12.

12. Antonio Coronel, *Tales of Mexican California*, ed. Doyce B. Nunis Jr., trans. Diane de Avalle-Arce (Santa Barbara: Bellerophon Books, 1994), 53.

13. Hubert Howe Bancroft, *History of California* (San Francisco: History Company, 1886), 2:768.

14. For a discussion of Mexican Californian architecture, see Richard B. Rice,

William A. Bullough, and Richard J. Orsi, *The Elusive Eden: A New History of California*, 3rd ed. (Boston: McGraw-Hill, 2002), 165. An excellent photo of the Coronel adobe, taken by "Godfrey" and entitled "Covered Sidewalk Near the Plaza," can be found in the Los Angeles Public Library Photo Collection (Call Number LAPL00008123). The image is viewable online at http://jpg1.lapl.org/00008/00008123.jpg.

15. "The Drama on the Pacific . . . Number 2", April 29, 1855.

16. Ibid.

17. Ibid.

18. The characterization of economies and cultures as "gift-exchange" (as opposed to "market exchange") is a distinction borrowed from anthropology. The first to fully theorize this idea was Marcel Mauss, in *The Gift: Form and Functions of Exchange in Archaic Societies*, trans. Ian Cunnison (1925; Glencoe, Ill.: Free Press, 1954.)

19. Peter Davis, "Plays and Playwrights to 1800," in *The Cambridge History of American Theatre*, vol. 1, ed. Don B. Wilmeth and Christopher Bigsby (New York: Cambridge University Press, 1998), 217.

20. Spain's American colonies, like those of other European powers, were conceived as sources of raw materials and markets for European-made products. Within such systems, manufacturing or independent trading interests were discouraged. See Steven W. Hackel, "Land, Labor, and Production: The Colonial Economy of Spanish and Mexican California," in *Contested Eden: California before the Gold Rush*, ed. Ramón Gutiérrez and Richard J. Orsi (Berkeley: University of California Press, 1998), 113.

21. Douglas Monroy, *Thrown among Strangers: The Making of Mexican Culture in Frontier California* (Berkeley: University of California Press, 1990), 100–102.

22. Marvin Carlson, *Places of Performance: The Semiotics of Theatre Architecture* (Ithaca, N.Y.: Cornell University Press, 1989), 41.

23. Ibid., 40.

24. Ibid., 41.

25. Richard Henry Dana, *Two Years before the Mast*, 1840, reprinted with foreword by James D. Hart (New York: Random House, 1936), 254.

26. "The Drama on the Pacific ... Number 2", April 29, 1855.

27. See *Orlando Furioso: A New Verse Translation*, trans. David R. Slavitt (Cambridge: Belknap Press of Harvard University Press, 2009), ix.

28. The stock character of the braggart soldier—"boasting, vainglorious, and mercenary"—had its roots in Greek New Comedy, and achieved iconic status with Roman playwright Plautus' *Miles Gloriosus* (ca. 206 BCE), whose lead character lent his name to the type. See Margarete Bieber, *The History of the Greek and Roman Theater* (1939; Princeton, N.J.: Princeton University Press, 1961), 150.

29. William Barnes Rhodes, *Bombastes Furioso: A Burlesque Tragic Opera* (London: Thomas Rodd, 1830), 11.

30. Ibid., 33.

31. For details, visit http://thelatc.org/encuentro2014/.

Setting Their Sites on Satire

The Algonquin Round Table's Non-Theatrical Spaces of Creative Genesis

Christine Woodworth

On a warm summer afternoon in 1933,[1] a small rowboat full of tourists landed on the shore of Neshobe Island in the tiny Lake Bomoseen near Castleton, Vermont. While enjoying a picnic lunch on the beach, the tourists were interrupted by an ax-wielding, mud-smeared naked man in a red fright wig who screamed and chased them back to their boat. This seemingly crazed person was none other than Harpo Marx who was, rather enthusiastically, preserving the isolation and privacy of the island, which was owned and populated by a special group of friends. Marx recollects, "I volunteered to deal with the interlopers. I stripped off all my clothes, put on my red wig, smeared myself with mud, and went whooping and war-dancing down to the shore, making Gookies[2] and brandishing an ax. The tourists snatched up their things, threw them into the boat, and rowed away fast enough to have won the Poughkeepsie Regatta. That put an end to the snooping that season. It also, I'm sure, started some juicy new rumors about our crazy goings-on."[3] The "crazy goings-on" alluded to by Marx were the antics of the iconic theatrical and literary wits of the Algonquin Round Table.

The prevailing image of the denizens of the Round Table more often than not situated them in the refined urban space of the Algonquin Hotel's elegant Rose Room. Indeed, dozens of comic illustrations portray them seated around the table, where they ate, drank, and vivaciously (or viciously, depending on one's perspective) discussed the theatrical and literary events of the day.[4] While their matrices of connection were initially forged around the table in the Rose Room, other non-theatrical spaces of camaraderie, whimsy, and debauchery, including Neshobe Island and Neysa McMein's painting studio, fueled creative theatrical genesis for the Algonquin Round Table and its hangers-on. An examination of the atmosphere and activities of these three social spaces—the Algonquin Hotel, Neshobe Island, and McMein's studio—offers a glimpse of the ways in which the spatial and social dynamics of the Round Table impacted the American theatre.

The members of the Algonquin Round Table offered myriad direct and indirect contributions to the theatre of the 1920s and early 1930s. Round Table gatherings in non-theatrical social spaces profoundly shaped theatre on countless stages in New York City and beyond. Their festive and ruthless get-togethers in a number of venues generated theatrical criticism as well as theatrical production, transforming these spaces into sites of critical and creative genesis. By examining locations of collaboration and contestation outside of traditional theatres, seemingly benign social sites can be recast as charged spaces of creation that are essential to theatre-making. Additionally, the Round Table's non-theatrical venues were simultaneously spaces of theatrical inclusion, as collaborative partnerships were forged, and exclusion, as some artists and productions were panned and reviled. These non-theatrical social spaces were the points of origin for the Round Table's impact on the theatre. The aftershocks of their theatrical influence are still felt today.

An extraordinary number of the Round Table wits wrote theatre criticism for one of the over fifteen daily newspapers in New York in the 1920s. Yet their contributions to theatre history extended far beyond print journalism. Kevin C. Fitzpatrick asserts: "The single unifying element among almost all members of the Round Table was the live theater business. Sitting at the table at any given point was at least one person who made his or her living on Broadway. Some wrote the shows that others acted, while across the table critics lay in wait to tear both of them down. Press agents drummed up publicity and ticket sales, so they sat next to the newspaper columnist who needed backstage gossip for the next day's edition. Directors and producers, the men behind the scenes, were among the most powerful in the city. Young actresses floated into the hotel dining room and held their own at the table."[5]

Documenting their own interactions and influence was clearly not at the forefront of Round Table members' minds in the midst of these social settings. As a result, limited artifacts have survived to reconstruct these gatherings. Yet what remains does afford intriguing possibilities for recovery and interpretation. Recently, theatre historians have worked to recover the labor and processes of artists, craftspeople, and technicians that have customarily been hidden or obscured to preserve the so-called magic of theatre.[6] By making visible the invisible labor and rewriting historical narratives to reflect that unseen work, theatre historians have revealed the toil and artistry of figures that may have been historically marginalized because of the nature of their jobs or because of other facets of their identities. This recovery work presents innumerable archival and historiographical challenges. How might this recovery trend and its methodologies extend to an examination of the non-theatrical spaces whose environs and interactions brought to bear countless theatrical collaborations for the Round Table? James Traub argues: "Theater is, of course, an inherently collaborative medium, but what is still remarkable about the [vicious] circle[7] of the 1920s is the extent to which they *were* a circle—a group of people who lived an almost collective life and whose work was in many ways, the record of that charmed, overheated, fiercely competitive society. It was the special privilege and delight of the audience, both in theaters and in living rooms across the country, to eavesdrop on this wicked and inspired conversation."[8] Exploring the Round Table's spaces of social camaraderie, and the atmosphere created therein, presents exciting—and daunting—methodological considerations. The physical remains of these spaces bear little resemblance to the sites where the Round Table assembled in the 1920s, as they have been renovated and remodeled over time. We are left with accounts of these gathering spaces and their occupants that have been preserved in memoirs and autobiographies. Countering these recollections are newspaper articles and columns by writers outside of the Round Table, who offer a more removed and critical perspective of the reputation of the Algonquin figures and the effect of their social gatherings on the theatre of their day.

The precise origins of the Algonquin Round Table have themselves become the stuff of folklore. Some scholars assert that tenacious theatre critic Alexander Woollcott began the gathering by inviting friends to join him at the hotel for lunch one day.[9] The prevailing origin story, however, traces the beginnings of the daily gatherings to a trick played on Woollcott. In 1919, press agents John Peter Toohey and Murdock Pemberton lured Woollcott to the Algonquin under the guise of decadent pastries with the ulterior motive to persuade him to write favorably about Eugene O'Neill. Woollcott abruptly dismissed their request and instead spent the remainder of lunch sharing stories of his own World War I escapades. In retribution for this, Toohey and Pemberton organized another lunchtime gathering of Woollcott's friends and colleagues who were brought to the hotel to roast the bombastic critic.[10] What precisely happened during that lunch has largely been lost. But Margaret Case, daughter of the hotel's proprietor, Frank Case, recollected that as lunch was breaking up someone remarked, "Why don't we do this every day?"[11] And indeed, they did.

The lunchtime gatherings initially were held in the hotel's Pergola room, but in 1920 Case moved the witty set to the Rose Room.[12] A large round table was placed in the middle of the room, and Case eventually added a red velvet rope "to set off the Rose Room from celebrity lunch-time watchers," thus transforming the dining space into a site of social and artistic exclusion.[13] The membership of the Round Table included theatre critics, playwrights, directors, actors, press agents, novelists, and so forth.[14] Membership to the group and access to the hallowed space of the table was usually facilitated by an invitation from a current member. The conversation was fast-paced and full of clever statements, many of which have subsequently become immortalized.[15] The wits gathered for close to ten years; Andrew B. Harris asserts that the Algonquin Round Table was the "epicenter of Broadway banter . . . where the wits gathered to either talk up or talk down the shows."[16] The Rose Room was the actual and figurative space of theatrical taste making in the 1920s and 1930s.

In a 1945 essay entitled "The Myth of the Algonquin Round Table," George S. Kaufman refuted the notion that friends gathered "intent upon praising each other to the skies and rigidly damning the work of any upstart outsider." Instead, he asserted, "The Round Table members ate at the Algonquin because Frank Case was good enough to hold a table for them, and because it was fun. The jokes, as I recall, were rather good but completely unimportant. I cannot recall that a serious literary note was ever injected, and anyone who tried to inject one would have had a piece of lemon chiffon pie crammed down his throat."[17] Yet the notion that Algonquin Round Table members promoted the work of their own membership persisted. A 1926 comic by John Held Jr. that was printed in the *New Yorker* features a group of eight men around a table, each scratching the back of the man[18] on his right. The caption for this image reads "Back Scratching at the Algonquin."[19] The notion that the wits of the vicious circle gathered in this space to manufacture and facilitate each other's literary, journalistic, and theatrical successes was nothing new to readers of newspapers and periodicals. As early as May 27, 1922, O. O. McIntyre's "Bits of New York Life" column—which was syndicated in papers across the country—stated, "Greenwich Village calls members of the 'circle' log-rollers. They are accused of the knavish vice of 'backscratching.' And whether true or not, the belief is growing that they are banded together as puff-hucksters for members only."[20]

While the round table in the Rose Room was seen as the iconic space of the Round Table members, part of what made their effect on theatre so potent was the fact that they carried their camaraderie and collaborations into a number of other spaces outside the Algonquin too. A few blocks uptown from the hotel was Neysa McMein's art studio, located on 57th Street, near Carnegie Hall. McMein's international fame stemmed primarily from her work as a painter and illustrator. She created covers for the *Saturday Evening Post, Woman's Home Companion, The Ladies World, McClure's* and, most notably, *McCall's,* for which she was the exclusive cover artist from 1923 until 1938. Her studio was across the hall from the apartment where Dorothy Parker lived with her first husband, and it soon became the auxiliary meeting space of the Algonquin Round Table's vicious circle and its many acolytes. Stuart Y. Silverstein describes McMein's studio as "New York's leading salon of the time."[21] In addition to the famous literary figures of the Algonquin Round Table, McMein's salon was host to countless actors, musicians, artists, and playwrights. Marc Connelly recounts in his memoir: "The world in which we moved was small, but it was churning with a dynamic group of young people. . . . Neysa's studio on the northeast corner of Sixth Avenue and Fifty-seventh Street was crowded all day by friends who played games and chatted with their startlingly [*sic*] beautiful young hostess as one pretty girl model after another posed for the pastel head drawings that would soon delight the eyes of America on the covers [of] periodicals."[22] Woollcott similarly noted, "If you loiter in Neysa McMein's studio, the world will drift in and out."[23] He describes the denizens of her salon: "Over at the piano Jascha Heifetz and Arthur Samuels may be trying to find out what four hands can do in the syncopation of a composition never thus desecrated before. Irving Berlin is encouraging them. Squatted uncomfortably around an ottoman, Franklin P. Adams, Marc Connelly and Dorothy Parker will be playing cold hands to see who will buy dinner that evening. At the bookshelf Robert C. Benchley and Edna Ferber are amusing themselves vastly by thoughtfully autographing her set of Mark Twain for her."[24] In addition to Connelly and Woollcott, other theatre artists and performers who frequented McMein's salon (and potentially sampled her legendary bathtub gin) included Mary Pickford, Robert Sherwood, George S. Kaufman, Charlie Chaplin, Paul Robeson, George Gershwin, Moss Hart, Alfred Lunt, and Lynn Fontanne.[25] One of the most prominent—albeit infrequent—visitors to McMein's studio was Noël Coward, who was one of her closest friends. McMein was instrumental in directing press attention to Coward's work in the United States, as he recounts in his diaries.[26] Coward described the inhabitants of McMein's studio as "swimming round and in and out like rather puzzled fish in a dusty aquarium."[27]

McMein's studio reverberated with activity as models, actors, writers, and friends came and went, ate and drank, and played countless games with one another. The informal chaos of the studio space nurtured new friendships, romances, and countless creative collaborations. In the midst of this flurry, McMein played casual hostess while focusing determinedly on the easel in front of her. As Coward attested, "Neysa paid little or no attention to anyone except when they arrived or left, when, with a sudden spurt of social conscience, she would ram a paint-brush into her mouth and shake hands with a kind of disheveled politeness."[28] Ruth Gordon recollects, "People eddied around the studio and talked with each other or to, or at, or about, and then drifted off and were missed or not."[29] The afternoons and evenings at the studio (in addition to lunchtime gatherings at the Algonquin, weekly dinners at the brownstone of Ruth Hale and Heywood Broun, parties at "412" [the home of Jane Grant and Harold Ross], and long weekends away at Woollcott's country home) provided an environment ripe for creative genesis, as writers and musicians developed friendships and mischief, and a space in which to rehearse those collaborations. Jane Grant, who was instrumental in the creation of the *New Yorker*, participated in a series of interviews for the Academy Award–winning documentary on the Algonquin Round Table, created by Aviva Slesin. In the notes and transcripts of that interview, Grant asserted that McMein helped create performances for any occasion (birthdays, new jobs, sale of a manuscript) and that her studio was the space where the theatrical culmination of the Round Table's satire—a production called *No Sirree!*—was created and rehearsed.[30]

Created collectively by the Round Table members, the production had its genesis and development primarily in McMein's studio, although it opened in a conventional theatre space. On April 30, 1922, *No Sirree!*, "An Anonymous Entertainment by the Vicious Circle of the Hotel Algonquin," was mounted for one night only at the 49th Street Theatre, which had been built the previous year by the Shuberts. The production was a series of vignettes and musical numbers, which spoofed the Broadway theatre of the time.

A review published the next day in the *New York Times* noted that the cast primarily featured critics and playwrights and "the only well-known persons in the cast took minor parts."[31] Scant evidence has survived of this piece other than a facsimile of the playbill and a handful of reviews.[32] In describing actress Laurette Taylor's reviews published in the *New York Times*, playwright Marc Connelly recollects, "Laurette rolled up her sleeves and with serious gusto panned hell out of everyone connected with *No, Sirree*."[33] Taylor admonished, "I would advise them all to leave the stage before they take it up. A pen in their hands is mightier than God's most majestic words in their mouths."[34] It is understandable that an actress might relish an opportunity to turn the tables on the vicious circle and their legendary acid pens.

In spite of the comical vitriol of Taylor's two reviews, this was a well-attended, invitation-only event.[35] The audience was a veritable who's who of the New York theatre, including Florenz Ziegfeld, Samuel Shipman, and Lee Shubert. The sketches lampooned the writings of Shipman, A. A.

Milne, Zoe Akins, and Eugene O'Neill.[36] While the event was something of a closed affair for New York theatre circles, it echoed beyond the city as syndicated dispatches appeared in papers as far away as Leavenworth, Kansas, and Portsmouth, Ohio. Lucy Jeanne Price in her "New York Letter" column dubbed the event "the finest fun imaginable" and asserted that the spoof was crafted with "infinite delicacy and whole heartedness."[37] O. O. McIntyre's "New York Day-By-Day" column stated, "The truth is that the critics gave one of the most amusing performances of the entire year in New York."[38] From the exclusive creative space of McMein's studio to the select coterie audience of New York theatre elite, *No Sirree!* eventually reverberated beyond its own limited spheres. For one member of the Round Table, this production was life changing. Robert Benchley's performance of his "Treasurer's Report" sketch impressed Irving Berlin so much that he booked Benchley into his Music Box Revue, which eventually catapulted him into acting.[39] Larger-than-life critic Alexander Woollcott was also allegedly invited to return to the stage by Samuel Shipman in one of his plays.[40] *No Sirree!* inspired Connelly and Kaufman to create another musical revue called *The Forty-niners*, which was a flop, running for fifteen performances in November of that same year.[41]

Shortly after *No Sirree!*, Woollcott and nine friends (including McMein and Harpo Marx) purchased the seven-acre Neshobe Island for their private retreat. An escape from the casual chaos of McMein's salon and the animated fervor of the Algonquin, Neshobe Island soon became a space of play for the Round Table. Woollcott was undeniably the host. McMein's husband saw this as a major drawback to visiting the island with his wife and referred to Woollcott as the "Bashaw of Bomoseen and Nabob of Neshobe," describing his leadership of the group as a dictatorship.[42] In a 1939 profile of Woollcott in *Life*, the writer dubs him the "Lord of Neshobe" and notes that "his guests wear old clothes on land, sometimes none at all when swimming—the sight of huge Woollcott floating in the water has been described as 'majestic.'"[43] The formality required by the space of the Algonquin Hotel's Rose Room was jettisoned when Round Table members were on the island. Dorothy Parker was rumored to have spent an entire weekend wearing only her hat.[44] Clearly, Harpo Marx was not the only inhabitant known for taking off his clothes while on the island, as the members of the Round Table revealed much more than their wit to one another.

Whether at the Algonquin, in Neysa's studio, gathered in someone's home, or visiting the island, the Round Table members transformed their spaces into sites of camaraderie and play. When in the city, they were famous for playing poker and other card games as well as word games. While on Neshobe, croquet was largely the game of choice during the day with spirited word, card, and guessing games dominating the evening. The most popular game was Murder, which was part mystery, part role-playing, and part hide-and-seek.[45] The entire island could be transformed into a larger-than-life stage space for these various activities. Woollcott helmed each adventure much like a director might helm a theatre production. As *Life* noted: "The host herds his guests from cribbage board to bridge table to lawn where he plays a murderous variant on croquet."[46] As a 1938 article in the *Salt Lake Tribune* noted, "Vermonters on the near-by mainland are given the opportunity to watch the wits of Broadway cavort at games and work—mostly games, as the rotund Woollcott is a genius at organizing the guests in amazing concoctions of his own that invariably inspire intense competitions."[47] While the locals may have seen the island as a theatre and themselves as the audience to the antics of its inhabitants, according to Harpo Marx, Woollcott saw himself as the audience on the island. Marx recollects, "Neshobe Island was in fact a kind of theatre to Aleck, with a continuous show. Each dawn raised the curtain on a new scene, each season was a new act, and each year a new drama."[48]

These three iconic spaces of camaraderie and play among the wits of the Round Table set the stage for a number of theatrical collaborations. While *No Sirree!* remains one of the most iconic iterations of their creative genesis, countless other theatrical renderings owe a debt to the web of relationships and atmosphere of social interplay afforded by the Algonquin Hotel, Neysa McMein's studio, and the private residence on Neshobe Island. Some of these renderings left material traces in theatre history. Dozens and dozens of theatre reviews written by members such as Woollcott, Parker, Benchley, Broun, Kaufman, and Hale have survived, providing valuable archival evidence of the New York theatre in the 1920s and underscoring how these spaces of camaraderie and contestation were the catalysts for much criticism of the time. Theatrical careers were launched and supported by the various Algonquin wits, including Noël Coward's American success and Lynn Fontanne's US acting career. Members of the Round Table and their goings-on in these various gathering spaces were the inspiration for thinly veiled characters in plays—including McMein, who was said to have inspired S. N. Berhman's 1932 play *Biography*, and Alexander Woollcott, who was famously dramatized in Kaufman and Hart's 1939 *The Man Who Came to Dinner*. Kaufman and Connelly wrote the play *Dulcy*, taking inspiration from a recurring character in one of Franklin Pierce Adams' columns. *Dulcy* was commissioned as a vehicle for Lynn Fontanne—eventually a regular visitor herself to McMein's studio and Neshobe. McMein herself created the cover art for the published edition of the play. Connelly and Kaufman went on to collaborate several more times, as did Kaufman and Edna Ferber; as Fitzpatrick argues, "At every stage of George S. Kaufman's career was a member of the Round Table."[49] And at every stage of Round Table membership, denizens of the vicious circle could be found in one of the myriad social spaces that set the stage for later collaborations.

Much of the residual influence of the Round Table's social spaces was ineffable and difficult to quantify or archive. Many writers of their time found the influence of the Algonquin wits troubling, as the earlier reference to the "back-scratching" comic suggests. A few years after referring to the Round Table as "puff-hucksters," O. O. McIntyre in his "New York Day by Day" column wrote of brewing tensions among the wits, predicting (inaccurately) that their demise as an organization was near. He wrote, "The so-called Algonquinites in reality represented a sprightly crew of young columnists, critics, playwrights and book reviewers. There were quite a number who had done noteworthy things in literature and the theater, but they were disposed to take themselves too seriously. So a myth grew up about them. And they were caught in a false glitter. Perhaps the chief beneficiary of the entire Algonquin affair is Frank Case, the proprietor, a personable fellow whose restaurant receipts have been amazingly enhanced by the publicity. It fills his dining rooms."[50] Similarly, when asked for a newspaper article what he would do if he won the lottery, press agent Walter J. Kingsley indicated that he "would suppress the Algonquin Round Table and send the young wits out into the world for new material."[51] The theatrical, literary, and social influence of the Algonquin Round Table was undeniable as they transformed seemingly benign social sites into spaces of collaborative creation and critical contestation. As Traub asserts, "The effect of all this nonstop collaborating, chronicling, criticizing, lunching, and drinking was to push the art of the period in the direction dictated by the circle's collective sensibility: wit, speed, sparkle, savoir-faire."[52] The gathering spaces of the Round Table, including the Algonquin Hotel, Neysa McMein's studio, and Neshobe Island, created eclectic spaces of collaboration in which the boundaries between social circle and artistic creation were nebulous. Whether dressed to the nines in the Rose Room or dressed in nothing at all on Neshobe Island, the members of the Algonquin Round Table gathered in these charged spaces, weaving their personal lives, artistry, and criticism together seamlessly, shaping theatrical careers and cultural trends in profound ways. The reverberations of their influence can still be felt today as theatres continue to produce their plays, scholars look to their writing for clues to cultural and social expression of an earlier time, and snarky critics and bloggers aspire to the quips and bon mots of the Algonquinites in a more contemporary idiom.

Notes

1. John Baragwanath, *A Good Time Was Had* (New York: Appleton-Century-Crofts, 1962), 148.

2. "Gookie" was Marx's signature comic expression, in which he puffed out his cheeks, stuck out his tongue, and crossed his eyes. In his autobiography he describes the real-life inspiration for this, a man named Gookie who rolled cigars in a shop window on Lexington Avenue. When he was twelve, Marx took it upon himself to mimic the faces Gookie made when rolling cigars. Harpo Marx and Rowland Barber, *Harpo Speaks!*, 14th ed. (Pompton Plains, N.J.: Limelight Editions, 2007), 52–54.

3. Ibid., 215.

4. See Aviva Slesin Collection of Research and Production Materials for *The Ten-Year Lunch: The Wit and Legend of the Algonquin Round Table 1920s-1988*, New York Public Library for the Performing Arts, Dorothy and Lewis B. Cullman Center Billy Rose Theatre Division, New York, for clippings and facsimiles of most of these comics.

5. Kevin C. Fitzpatrick, *The Algonquin Round Table New York: A Historical Guide* (Guilford, Conn.: Lyons Press, 2015), 143.

6. See Elizabeth Osborne and Christine Woodworth, eds., *Working in the Wings: New Perspectives on Theatre History and Labor* (Carbondale, Ill.: Southern Illinois University Press, 2015); Christin Essin, *Stage Designers in Early Twentieth-Century America: Artists, Activists, Cultural Critics* (New York: Palgrave Macmillan, 2012); Timothy R. White, *Blue-Collar Broadway: The Craft and Industry of American Theater* (Philadelphia: University of Pennsylvania Press, 2015).

7. "Vicious circle" was another nickname for the Round Table.

8. James Traub, *The Devil's Playground: A Century of Pleasure and Profit in Times Square* (New York: Random House, 2005), 64.

9. Edwin P. Hoyt, *Alexander Woollcott: The Man Who Came to Dinner*, new ed. (Radnor, Pa.: Chilton Book Company, 1973), 132.

10. James R. Gaines, *Wit's End: Days and Nights of the Algonquin Round Table* (New York: Harcourt Brace Jovanovich, 1977), 58; Margot Peters, *Design for Living: Alfred Lunt and Lynn Fontanne, a Biography* (New York: Alfred A. Knopf, 2003), 22–24.

11. Ibid., 28.

12. Ethan Mordden, *The Guest List: How Manhattan Defined American Sophistication—from the Algonquin Round Table to Truman Capote's Ball* (New York: St. Martin's Press, 2010), 16.

13. Gaines, *Wit's End*, 133.

14. For a detailed account of the members of the Round Table, see Fitzpatrick, *The Algonquin Round Table New York*.

15. Hoyt, *Alexander Woollcott*, 133.

16. Andrew B. Harris, *Broadway Theatre* (London: Routledge, 1994), 12.

17. George S. Kaufman, "The Myth of the Algonquin Round Table," in *The*

Lost Algonquin Round Table: Humor, Fiction, Journalism, Criticism and Poetry From America's Most Famous Literary Circle, ed. Nat Benchley and Kevin C. Fitzpatrick (Bloomington, Ind.: iUniverse, 2009), 1.

18. The majority of these images are dominated by renderings of the male members of the Round Table set. While there were several women involved in the Round Table, they are outnumbered by the men in the cartoon in which they appear. In one instance, a cartoon bears a caption that describes the animated male figures individually while it offers a single woman who sits with her hat covering her eyes and her mouth closed. It reads, "The solitary lady, who seems awe-stricken by her surroundings, is a composite of the very few members of her sex who have been privileged to penetrate this literary arcanum." *Shadowland*, 1923, 38, Aviva Slesin Collection of Research and production Materials for *The Ten-Year Lunch: the Wit and Legend of the Algonquin Round Table*, Billy Rose Theatre Division, The New York Public Library.

19. Judith Yaross Lee, *Defining New Yorker Humor* (Jackson: University Press of Mississippi, 2000), 169. See also Aviva Slesin Collection, New York Public Library.

20. O. O. M'Intyre, "Bits of New York Life," *Atlanta Constitution*, May 27, 1922, 4.

21. Stuart Y. Silverstein, "Introduction," *Not Much Fun: The Lost Poems of Dorothy Parker* (New York, Scribner, 2009), 29.

22. Marc Connelly, *Voices Offstage: A Book of Memoirs* (New York: Holt, Rinehart and Winston, 1968), 81.

23. Alexander Woollcott, *Enchanted Aisles* (New York: G. P. Putnam's Sons, 1924), 36.

24. Ibid.

25. Silverstein, "Introduction," 29; Gaines, *Wit's End*, 77–78.

26. Noël Coward, *The Noël Coward Diaries*, ed. Graham Payn and Sheridan Morley (New York: Da Capo Press, 1982), 57.

27. Quoted in Baraganath, *A Good Time Was Had*, 78.

28. Ibid.

29. Ruth Gordon, *Myself among Others* (New York: Atheneum, 1971), 342.

30. Aviva Slesin Collection, New York Public Library, box 2, folder 2.

31. "Critics Are Actors to Actor Audience," *New York Times*, May 1, 1922.

32. For an account of the historiographical challenges surrounding this event and a reconstruction of the performance, see Jay Malarcher, "*No Sirree!* A One-Night Stand with the Algonquin's Vicious Circle," in *Art, Glitter, and Glitz: Mainstream Playwrights and Popular Theatre in 1920s America*, ed. Arthur Gewirtz and James Kolb (Westport, Conn.: Praeger Publishers, 2004), 147–58.

33. Connelly, *Voices Offstage*, 89.

34. Laurette Taylor, "Actress Gets Back at the Critics," *New York Times*, May 1, 1922, 22.

35. Malarcher, "*No Sirree!* A One-Night Stand with the Algonquin's Vicious Circle," 150.

36. Gaines, *At Wit's End*, 63; Felicia Hardison Londré, "Twitting O'Neill: His

Plays of the 1920s Subjected to `La Critique Créatrice,'" *Eugene O'Neill Review* 26 (2004): 118–43.

37. Lucy Jeanne Price, "New York Letter," *Leavenworth Times*, May 9, 1922, 4.

38. O. O. McIntyre, "New York Day-By-Day," *Portsmouth Daily Times*, May 18, 1922, 16. In 1922 the title of the column was printed with hyphens, however, in 1925 (see note 50) the column title contained no hyphens.

39. Gaines, *At Wit's End*, 66.

40. O. O. McIntyre, "New York Day-By-Day," 16.

41. Burns Mantle, *The Best Plays of 1922–1923* (Boston: Small, Maynard & Company, 1923), 9.

42. Baragwanath, *A Good Time Was Had*, 147.

43. "Life Goes Calling on Alexander Woollcott," *Life*, October 30, 1939, 87.

44. Peters, *Design for Living*, 122.

45. Marx and Barber, *Harpo Speaks!*, 218–19.

46. "Life Goes Calling," 87.

47. "Master of Island Retreat Tries Croquet," *Salt Lake Tribune*, August 21, 1938, 20.

48. Marx and Barber, *Harpo Speaks!*, 213–14.

49. Fitzpatrick, *The Algonquin Round Table New York*, 43.

50. O. O. McIntyre, "New York Day By Day," *Times Herald* (Olean, N.Y.), August 15, 1925, 24. In 1922 the title of the column was printed with hyphens (see notes 38 and 41), however, in 1925 the column title contained no hyphens.

51. "When Your Dream Materializes, How Will You Deport Yourself?," *Oakland Tribune Magazine*, May 24, 1925, 94.

52. Traub, *The Devil's Playground*, 64.

Struggling to Stage

The Contentious Issue
of Theatre Space in Kolkata

Arnab Banerji

The question of space assumes special significance in the case of the popular Bengali group theatre practiced in Kolkata, India. Theatre companies, referred to as groups in this theatre culture, do not own or control any of the spaces that are used in any aspect of the performance process, depending entirely on rental resources. This results in a unique performative circumstance that makes theatre-making a challenging "business" in this Eastern Indian city. In this essay, I trace a brief trajectory of the Bengali group theatre genre of performance, followed by an examination of the way theatres are spread out in the city of Kolkata, and the spatial idiosyncrasies of these theatre spaces. Using the work of Ric Knowles and Gay McAuley I demonstrate the challenges that space—or the lack thereof—creates for Bengali theatre practitioners.

Amidst the acute shortage of performance spaces and the resultant competition amongst groups to secure a spot to perform are a few groups like Alternative Living Theatre, Swabhav Kolkata, and Theatre Formation Paribartak. These groups have deliberately chosen to steer clear of the space war by looking for alternative spaces for both rehearsal and performance. In doing so, they are not only attempting to point a way out of the jostling for space that threatens to sap a large share of their creative energy, but they are also able to stage their shows more regularly and at a relatively lower cost, thus circumventing two of the biggest challenges facing Bengali theatre groups today. I reference here the work of one such group, Theatre Formation Paribartak (henceforth TFP), to demonstrate how this company has managed to eke out a space of their own in the Kolkata performance landscape.[1]

Bengali group theatre is the most popular theatre form practiced in Kolkata, West Bengal, India. It traces its roots to the progressive theatre movement that gained currency amongst the Bengali middle class in the 1930s. The first groups emerged from the ruins of the Indian Peoples' Theatre Association (IPTA) after this erstwhile cultural front of the Communist Party of India disintegrated, following the party being declared illegal in 1948 by the Indian National Congress-led federal government.[2]

The newly created groups produced plays that demanded technical and aesthetic rigor. The groups turned to Sanskrit classics as well as to the dramatic works of the Bengali poet Rabindranath Tagore for inspiration and subject matter. This was in sharp contrast to the exclusively political and socially conscious theatre that the predecessor of the group theatre, the IPTA, was producing. The shift from the political to the quest for an aesthetic beauty and complexity led to creative and political differences among group members. The disagreement over the purpose of theatre coupled with the culturally conditioned Bengali tendency of *daladali* (group-ism) resulted in fissures within the groups during and through the mid-1960s.[3]

Personality clashes more than political differences seem to be the main reason that most groups disintegrated and continue to disintegrate. The personality clash might be between the director and other members, or among the actors within the group.[4] It is quite likely that a popular or famous member of the group might gather around him or her a group of sycophants to "carve out a new area of power," leading to the breakup of the old group and the formation of a new one.[5] The splits usually follow one of two models. The first exists when ordinary members of the group decide to quit the parent organization to form newer groups, examples of which include groups like Rupakar, Theatre Workshop, and Sudrak. The second happens when the director of a group leaves with a band of loyal associates to form a new group. Theatre groups Nandimukh and Anya Theatre were created in this way when revered actor-director Ajitesh Bandyopadhyay left Nandikar with some associates in 1977, and noted director Bibhas Chakraborty did the same upon leaving Theatre Workshop in 1985.[6]

By the 1970s—over twenty years after the first group, Bohurupee, was formed in 1948—there were more than a dozen theatre outfits competing for space and visibility in Calcutta.[7] The growing number of groups also found support in the increasing foothold of leftist thought in mainstream politics in the state of West Bengal after four years of underground political activity by Indian communists following independence. By the time the Left Front, led by the Communist Party of India (Marxist), was elected to power in 1977 for an uninterrupted thirty-four years of governance, the Bengali group theatre had firmly established itself as the preeminent theatre form in the city of Kolkata.[8]

Kolkata is situated on the banks of the river Hooghly in Eastern India. Unlike New York or London, Kolkata does not have a theatre district at present. At the turn of the twentieth century, during the heyday of commercial theatre in the city, North Kolkata boasted a series of performance venues with companies competing for patronage and clientele.[9] At present, however, most of the theatre buildings in North Kolkata have fallen into disrepair. With the expansion and growth of the city, theatre buildings, too, have left their North Kolkata moorings and are now spread across the city. The theatre halls in Kolkata can be divided into several sub-categories based on location and ownership.

Theatres are roughly located in three broad geographic areas of the city—North, Central, and South—and they are either privately owned or administered by the state government. At present, there are a total of seven well-known venues that guarantee some form of financial return and visibility to the theatre groups, meaning that over a hundred theatre groups compete for these seven performance venues. The groups also have to deal with the attendant politics and corruption regarding securing reservations and the constant rise in costs, thanks to an ever-increasing demand and supply curve between available performance spaces and performance groups in Kolkata. The scramble for space creates a unique style in which performers and companies negotiate with what, where, and how they perform.

Ananda Lal, defining the Bengali group theatre writes, "Making a virtue of their poverty, groups register as non-profit organizations. . . . Most [groups] have a hand-to-mouth existence, scraping together tiny budgets from one production to the next."[10] The poverty that plagues Bengali group theatre is the reason that no single group owns or controls its own performance space. Ric Knowles has used the moniker "nomadic and touring theatre" to describe similar itinerant companies in the English-language theatre world. There is, however, a significant difference between the companies that Knowles has in mind and Bengali group theatre companies. English-language companies like Cheek by Jowl, Ex Machina, and Theatre Complicite begin the search for a new space at the conclusion of a run, whereas Bengali group theatre companies must load in and strike for every single performance.

In addition to such limited access to performance spaces, the problem is further compounded by the fact that theatre groups in Kolkata seldom own or control any space where the processes of production take place. One such example is the rehearsal hall, where, as Ric Knowles points out, almost eighty percent of the creative process takes place.[11] Despite this, it is the space over which a theatre group usually has the least amount of control, and it is seldom considered a creative space in the design of a show.[12] Some groups even move from one space to another depending on availability and affordability. The rehearsal process for TFP's December 2012 production of Sukumar Ray's *Lakkhaner Shaktishel* (The Fatal Attack on Lakshmana) began in such a nomadic fashion. The group assembled in multiple locations for cold readings and the initial blocking. Finally, the company decided to take advantage of the mild Kolkata autumn/winter and hold rehearsals on a cast member's rooftop.

The nomadic quality of preparing for a production leads to exhaustion, which is the result of the physical strain of having to adjust continually to a new rehearsal space. The fact that the stage picture being attempted is hardly ever fully visualized before the production moves onto the actual playing space also contributes to creative exhaustion. Several directors, like Suman Mukhopadhyay, complain about the unavailability of dates in city auditoriums either for rehearsals or shows and the problems that this shortage of space gives rise to in the creative process.[13] TFP's rehearsal process has offered the company some respite from this creative exhaustion by locating an alternative and cost-effective rehearsal space. However, the solution appears temporary. It is almost impossible to work outdoors in Kolkata during the significantly warmer spring months of February and March, which lead into the stifling heat of summer, followed by the incessant downpours during the monsoon season. In addition, TFP's process does not circumvent the problem of the final stage picture not being realized until the show's opening.

The location of the rehearsal space, ease of access via public transport, and security all impact the people involved with the theatre. Gay McAuley reminds us that actors often have to put up with work conditions that would "provoke strike action in other workplaces."[14] McAuley's assertion gains even more currency in the context of the Bengali group theatre where work conditions are seldom conducive to a productive process. Bengali group theatre, however, carries an ideological baggage that presumes theatre work is not merely entertaining but also socially productive. The largely unpaid performers, therefore, feel morally obligated to press on in spite of trying (and often downright horrible) working conditions.[15] The voluntary nature of participation in theatre thus negates the possibility of an expressed adverse reaction substantially. The frustration of not being able to address this situation adds further strain on already exhausted practitioners.

Lack of affordable and suitable rehearsal space affects not only the quality but also the quantity of theatre produced in Kolkata. Likewise, it determines to a large extent what kind of theatre is produced. Young, inexperienced, experimental, and avant-garde groups often find it difficult to afford the space and time for rehearsals. These restrictions lead to a situation where, according to McAuley, the laws of the market determine "whose voice may be heard in the theatre."[16] The workings of these market forces can be seen in action in recent years. The recognizable Bengali group theatres have resorted to regurgitating formulaic plays, whereas newer and younger groups are finding it difficult to eke out space to rehearse and produce experimental works. Although groups like Swabhav Kolkata and TFP have experimented with rehearsal spaces, the imbalance between the demand and supply of production spaces has impeded the growth of experimental theatre in Kolkata.[17]

Adverse work conditions not only plague the production process but also extend to performance spaces. Most theatre auditoriums in Kolkata are multi-purpose venues, with theatre shows being just one of the many types of events hosted in the buildings. Therefore, the halls do not cater to the specialized needs of theatre. This lack of distinct theatrical purpose affects both practitioners and audiences. The auditoriums are therefore not empty spaces waiting for new productions to be mounted, but containers replete with "ghostings" from alternate uses.[18] Ghostings arise out of previous experiences and associations that the audience and even those who produce theatre have with a particular space. Groups like TFP have demonstrated effective uses of "ghosted" space by mounting productions in venues that are significant cultural markers, like the erstwhile palace of the landed gentry or a railway station, challenging normal theatrical conventions. However, most groups have to deal with problems common to "ghosted" spaces in Kolkata. For example, auditoriums are only minimally rigged and equipped for lighting instruments since a political meeting or an award ceremony does not require extensive lighting design. Similarly, since most of the other events held in these theatre spaces are easier to amplify, the auditoriums are not acoustically well equipped, either.

In addition to the physical limitations of temporary theatrical performance venues, it is challenging to design such a space and its surroundings to facilitate the psychological arousal of the audience. Gay McAuley draws on psychological studies of space to point out a connection between what is termed the "information rate" of an environment and the psychological arousal levels of the inhabitants and users of the space. The information rate of a space is the ease with which it can be accessed and the ways in which a space is presented and perceived. Common factors that determine the information rate of a building are the color of the walls, the décor, the lighting, and cleanliness.[19] If the information rate for a building is low (characterized by dull wall color and careless lighting and décor), the space is perceived as either bland or boring and users tend to be understimulated. In addition to the performance space, other parts of the audience space—constituting the foyer, lobby, refreshment stands, stairways and corridors that lead to the auditorium, and box office—all contribute to the information rate of a theatre space. Theatre spaces in Kolkata suffer from low information rate because neither the management nor the groups performing in the spaces make an effort to add to the information rate of the spaces.

To enhance the space, theatre groups in Kolkata will sometimes set up small displays in the theatre lobby that highlight past achievements, including press reviews and a few photographs from the group's most recent productions. The small displays showcase the group but do not engage with the particular space in which the performance is being held. Therefore, the displays never quite integrate with the space, but serve as superficial marketing tools for the group. Groups are reluctant to invest any more than the small displays to dress the lobby space. Having to dismantle everything at the end of every performance and then painstakingly set it up again for any subsequent performances is certainly a major deterrent. Administrators of these multi-use buildings seem equally reluctant to decorate the audience space because the number of people coming to the theatre does not affect their business.[20]

Given the importance of the audience experience, TFP has recognized the need to increase the information rate for spaces that their audience does not associate with being theatre spaces. To this end, the company has taken care to make the performance space and adjoining social spaces welcoming to the audience. In the case of their December 2012 production of Sukumar Ray's *Lakkhaner Shaktishel*, the audience was greeted by the soothing warm blue glow of the pre-show lighting and offered a cool drink in earthen tumblers. Ushers dressed in military fatigues were stationed along the various routes to the performance venue to ensure that the audience did not get lost navigating the confusing North Kolkata lanes, and also to welcome them into the world of the play, set in a military camp. The venue itself, however, lacked adequate audience amenities, since it was not a custom-built auditorium.

While food and drinks are often perceived to be typical amenities within theatre spaces, food and drinks are not allowed inside auditoriums in Kolkata.[21] Although drinks were served to audience members who attended *Lakkhaner Shaktishel*, this is an unusual example within the Bengali theatre. Part of the reason for disregarding the connection between food and theatre in Kolkata might be that Bengalis tend to eat dinner late, and thus it is expected that most people will only snack while at the theatre rather than enjoy a meal at a restaurant attached to (or near) the auditorium.

There is, however, no plausible reason for ignoring the possible revenue that having a snack counter attached to the theatre could generate. The negligence stems from the fact that theatre is not considered part of the leisure industry in Kolkata, but rather is seen as a cerebral exercise. What the audience pays for is not necessarily a good night out, but an intellectually stimulating evening with entertainment taking a secondary role.[22]

Beyond the areas reserved for the audience are the spaces that practitioners consider to be private—the domain of their work and the space where their craft is practiced. McAuley observes that writing about this area of the theatre is especially difficult since it has not been systematically documented and the area continues to be considered private by practitioners.[23] The backstage is the "world of work," accessible only to those who have the requisite skills to make it work.[24] The effort to maintain the privacy of practitioner space can be the result, as McAuley notes, of concealing the sordid nature of the work environment provided for actors and production staff.[25] However, the contrast between front of the house and backstage is not as stark in Kolkata. The negligence of the theatre hall administrators affects every part of the space, and thus both audience spaces and practitioner spaces often bear a forlorn look. In the case of a site-specific performance, like TFP's *Lakkhaner Shaktishel*, the performance space presented a conundrum of sorts. While the venue was one of the group's choosing, lack of financial resources meant the company could not customize the space to meet all the needs of the performers. The company had to improvise storage, operator's booths, and dressing rooms. In particular, the dressing room is an important part of the practitioner space in a theatre, as both McAuley and Knowles acknowledge.[26] They suggest that allocation of private dressing rooms is an important marker of a particular actor's position in the theatre company. The absence of private dressing rooms in Kolkata theatres leads to an increased sense of community backstage. This is in keeping with the founding principles of the earliest Bengali group theatre groups, which strove to work against the star system and emphasized community building.[27] This was certainly true of the TFP production of *Lakkhaner Shaktishel* in which two rooms were converted to makeshift dressing rooms, one male and one female. The unavailability of adequately sized dressing rooms made quick changes in the absence of wings doubly difficult. Lack of mirrors and proper lighting meant that actors had to guess about possible looks while applying makeup, all of which led to compromised choices.[28] For example, the director had to eliminate the original plan for a couple of quick changes, and the costume director and makeup supervisor were asked to keep makeup and costumes to a minimum and without complications in keeping with the state of the available practitioner space.

Experience has taught Bengali group theatre actors to negotiate with backstage spaces in most theatres where shows are held regularly. However, this is not true in the case of experimental work like that done by TFP, or when a performance group has to travel outside Kolkata. The conditions of backstage spaces, and especially dressing rooms, vary widely. As little as is predictable in Kolkata, virtually nothing is under the group's control for touring performances known as "call shows," which run from October through February. During this season, Kolkata-based groups are often invited to showcase their latest productions at suburban theatre festivals, fairs, and other community events. If the show is being held in a theatre, the group has access to dressing rooms, but these dressing rooms often leave a lot to be desired. In still other places where the groups have to perform on makeshift stages, there is often only a tarpaulin-covered space for costume changes.

Theatre, Knowles reminds us, is the most social and place-specific among the arts.[29] The continuous displacement that Bengali theatre groups endure in order to stage their shows results in a loss of that specificity. Having to negotiate with continuous displacement, practitioners of Bengali theatre create performances that cater to universal themes and ideas. This compromise negates significant engagement with any particular performance venue; companies resort to adjustments instead. While the performances (mostly) take place in the same city and are attended by audiences that belong to a similar (if not identical) milieu, moving a performance across venues requires subtle and often more definitive tweaks in both performance and design. Veteran scenic designer Khaled Choudhuri remembers one such instance when the director Shyamanand Jalan of Padatik decided to saw off a portion of the set for *Evam Indrajit*, which Choudhuri had designed.[30] This decision significantly changed the look of the play, but Jalan defended his choice, saying that it did not affect the meaning of the play. Similarly arbitrary changes were made by the theatre group Rang-Roop when director Sima Mukhopadhyay dictated the way the set was to be arranged hours before a performance without prior consultation with the designer.[31] Such last-minute changes, in turn, significantly affect audience reception. Audiences for Bengali group theatre shows get attuned to looking for universal messages in the plays they see. For example, *Mayer Moto* (Like a Mother) is about loving and being devoted to aging parents, and *Dui Hujurer Goppo* (The Tale of Two Gentlemen) is about corrupt and pompous Bengali gentry. The story takes center stage over the aesthetic choices made in its presentation. When the work of the designers and collaborative leadership of the director take a backseat over the story, it is frustrating to artists and detrimental to experimentation in both content and form.

As chronicled here, the exhaustion of a nomadic style of performance plagues the Bengali group theatre in multiple ways. Some of the exhaustion is on the surface, like the exhaustion of having to continually look for a space and not being able to control the space when it is found. Other types of exhaustion are subliminal and affect the look and feel of the theatre culture. The continuous displacement takes a toll on the physical set. Actors, directors, and technicians are fatigued from having to negotiate with a new space for each performance. The lack of rootedness prompts theatre practitioners to make creative compromises in order to keep producing theatre. These compromises lead to revisiting and reusing formulas which have worked in the past, encompassing narrative, design, and performance. The overuse of formulas contributes in turn to the whole theatre culture having a dated, weary feel. By choosing to step outside the vicious cycle imposed by spatial constraints on both the quantity and the quality of theatre work in Kolkata, groups like Theatre Formation Paribartak are creating new spaces for experimental theatre. It is perhaps only by thinking outside the box, as TFP demonstrates, that Bengali group theatre can and will be able to escape the challenges imposed by an acute shortage of performance spaces.

Notes

1. For the reflection on the works of TFP, I rely here on my own observations and notes made during a year-long research trip and creative collaboration with the group in 2012 and 2013 in Kolkata, India.

2. See Darsan Chaudhuri, *Gananatya Andolan* (Kolkata: Anustup, 2009).

3. See Kuntal Mukhopadhyay, *Theatre and Politics: A Study of Group Theatre Movement of Bengal, 1948–1987* (Calcutta: Bibhasa, 1999), for a more detailed and nuanced discussion on the inherent groupism in the Bengali culture and its effect on the Bengali theatre.

4. Ibid.

5. Ibid., 143.

6. Ibid., 144.

7. The name of the city of Calcutta was changed to a more traditional Bengali-sounding Kolkata in 2000. I use both names in this essay to signify the confusion surrounding the colonial/post-colonial identity of the city space.

8. The Communist Party of India was legalized in 1952 and allowed to participate in India's first-ever general elections in 1952. The party split into two principal factions, the Communist Party of India and the Communist Party of India (Marxist), in 1964 over the party's stance during the 1961 Sino-India conflict. The newly formed CPI (M) found electoral favor in the elections of 1967 and emerged as a major political force in Kerala, Tripura, and West Bengal, the three states that

have traditionally been leftist strongholds. The left movement suffered a major setback during the emergency imposed by the Indira Gandhi–led Federal government in 1971. The emergency period witnessed the suspension of civil rights and liberties of the average citizen and severe political repression unleashed on the opposition. The 1972 elections in West Bengal resulted in a landslide victory for the centrist Congress Party amidst allegations that no electoral protocol had been followed. In spite of efforts by the state and federal governments, the CPI (M) and its left allies held their ground and emerged victorious in the state elections of 1977, winning 243 out of the 291 seats in the West Bengal state legislature. The CPI (M)–led Left Front won six subsequent terms (totaling thirty-four years) before being ousted by the Mamata Banerjee–led Trinamool Congress in 2011. For a more detailed account on the history of the Communist Party in India see "How the Left Front and Its Government Emerged," on the website of CPI (M), W.B. State Committee, http://www.cpimwb.org.in/history.php. Also see Kiranmoy Raha, *Bengali Theatre* (Calcutta: National Book Trust, 1978), and Sushil Kumar Mukherjee, *The Story of the Calcutta Theatres, 1753–1980* (Calcutta: K. P. Bagchi, 1982), for a detailed timeline of Bengali theatre.

9. For a detailed discussion on the public/commercial theatre in Kolkata, see Raha, *Bengali Theatre*, and Mukherjee, *The Story of the Calcutta Theatres*.

10. Ananda Lal, *The Oxford Companion to Indian Theatre* (New Delhi: Oxford, 2004), 139.

11. Ric Knowles, *Reading the Material Theatre* (Cambridge: Cambridge University Press, 2004), 67.

12. Ibid.

13. Suman Mukhopadhyay, in discussion with the author, June 5, 2013.

14. Ibid.

15. See Mukhopadhyay, *Theatre and Politics*, for a detailed discussion on the voluntary nature of participation in the Bengali group theatre and its amateur nature.

16. Ibid.

17. Young directors and actors from groups like Mad About Drama (M.A.D) and Hypokrites complain about the repetition of formulas and the unavailability of production as well as performance spaces for their creative work. See "Kolkataye Anyorokom Jubora," *Natya Mukhopotro* 862, November 11, 2012. The title of the article can be translated as "Youths with a Difference in Kolkata."

18. Marvin Carlson claims that "the 'something else' that a performance space was before (or in this case is still), like the body of the actor that exists before, is interpellated into a character, and has the potential, often realized, of 'bleeding through' the process of reception." See Marvin Carlson, *The Haunted Stage: The Theatre as Memory Machine* (Ann Arbor: University of Michigan Press, 2001), 133.

19. Gay McAuley, *Space in Performance* (Ann Arbor: University of Michigan Press, 2000), 59–60.

20. The groups have to pay a flat rental fee to use an auditorium. The auditoriums do not get a percentage of ticket sales.

21. There are some notable exceptions to this trend, but that discussion is beyond the scope of the present essay.

22. Any standard text on Bengali Theatre, such as Kiranmoy Raha's *Bengali Theatre* or Kuntal Mukhopadhyay's *Politics and Theatre*, discusses the intellectual as opposed to mere entertainment role played by the group theatre in Kolkata. The observations made in these critical texts are corroborated further by my own experience with and observation of this theatre culture since 2001.

23. McAuley, *Space in Performance*, 63–64.

24. Ibid.

25. Ibid., 65.

26. Ibid.; Knowles, *Reading the Material Theatre*, 69–70.

27. The predecessors of Bengali Group Theatre, the IPTA, focused on creating a performance culture that would emphasize community over the individual star. The vicious star system has gradually made its way back into the Bengali group theatre in the last two decades. However, the culture of not having separate dressing rooms for the principals in a play has been retained, probably because auditorium managers are reluctant to spend the money to redo the backstage area. Newer auditoriums like the GD Birla Sabhaghar, located in South Kolkata, have smaller dressing rooms, arguably for the leading company members. Bengali group theatre troupes mostly convert these spaces into communal dressing rooms, but I have worked with other companies that assigned the smaller rooms to individual actors.

28. The observations about the Theatre Formation Paribartak (TFP) production made throughout the essay are first-hand. I worked closely with the group during a yearlong field research trip to Kolkata, India, in 2012–2013.

29. Knowles, *Reading the Material Theatre*, 89.

30. Samik Bandyopadhyay and Pratibha Agarwal, ed., *Hindi Theatre in Kolkata: Shyamanand Jalan and His Times* (Calcutta: Natya Shodh Sansthan and Thema, 2011), 52.

31. I was a participating member of Rang-Roop between 2001 and 2009 and have continued to associate and work with the group. The observation made here is my own.

"For the Children"

Doyle and Debbie at The Station Inn; or, the Politics of Space in "The Gulch"

Chase Bringardner

On the south side of downtown Nashville, Music City USA, nestled in a bend on Interstate 40, sits a refreshed, repurposed, re-gentrified urban mixed-use neighborhood called "The Gulch." The Gulch is home to trendy condos, restaurants, organic groceries, and specialty stores aimed at encouraging a younger, wealthier demographic to move downtown. Once a "bustling railroad yard with origins dating to before the Civil War," The Gulch fell into "neglect and blight" following World War II until an urban revitalization initiative took hold in the early 2000s.[1] Today, The Gulch is, according to promotional materials, a "vibrant urban district and a popular local destination for shopping, dining and entertainment."[2] Those warehouses, industrial buildings, and railroad tracks have been replaced by high rises, high-concept eateries, and, of course, an Urban Outfitters (see figure 4).

According to the developer's website, "The Gulch is the only neighborhood in Nashville governed by a privately controlled land use Master Plan."[3] MarketStreet, a privately held real estate investment and development company, was designated the Master Developer of The Gulch by the city of Nashville in 2001, the only such designation in the city's history. As such, MarketStreet maintains and updates the so-called Gulch Master Plan, which, according to the website, "serves as a governing document guiding the future development patterns in the neighborhood."[4] The website proclaims that the most recent update of the neighborhood's strategic plan "envisions greater density than ever before, encompassing over 4,500 residential units, over 1.5 million square feet of commercial office space, and over a half million square feet of retail and restaurants."[5] And the development has simultaneously managed a stellar environmental record, being recognized in 2009 as the first LEED ND–certified green

Figure 4. The Gulch Development Project towers over The Station Inn. Nashville, Tennessee. Courtesy of Chase Bringardner.

neighborhood in the southeastern United States and only the fourth Silver Certified neighborhood in the world, achieving "international recognition for excellence among the finest developments incorporating the principles of smart growth, urbanism and sustainability."[6] Sounds like gentrified heaven in repurposed cowboy boots.

Yet at the epicenter of all this redevelopment sits a small, rather unassuming building with a stack stone, sandstone façade identifiable only by its signature, weathered red door, and a worn, square, plastic sign from the 1970s. Just inside the door, perched on a battered wooden stool, is an older gentleman with a grey metal cashbox. Admission to all Station Inn–produced shows is cash only and strictly on a first-come, first-serve basis with no reservations and no advance sales. Inside you find a 165-seat "club" with walls lined with old bus seats; a simple, rectangular stage against one wall; and long tables surrounded by dilapidated chairs, stuffing poking through torn faux leather. If you are hungry, you find the same offerings of popcorn, hot dogs, and pizza you would have found decades earlier. The entire experience feels as if you had stepped back in time into what has been described as "a 1970s rec room," with signage and layers of graffiti on the walls that support that conclusion.[7] You have entered a space in stark contrast to its larger location, The Gulch—a distant, defiant relic of an earlier, messier time.

Figure 5. The Station Inn. Nashville, Tennessee. Courtesy of Chase Bringardner.

The Station Inn, "Bluegrass and Roots Music's premiere listening room," was opened in Nashville by a group of six bluegrass pickers and singers in 1974.[8] After surviving a series of managers and a change in location in 1978, The Station Inn quickly established itself as one of the most important live music venues in Nashville, a frequent hangout for the elite of bluegrass and country musicians, including Bill Monroe and Allison Kraus. Yet today, The Station Inn occupies an incredibly perilous space within the shifting urban geography of a gentrifying Nashville (see figure 5). Precariously perched in the middle of incredibly valuable property, this unassuming, intimate structure, with that simple façade and seemingly original, illuminated plastic sign, still provides a critical venue for the development and popularization of bluegrass.[9] Yet despite its historical significance and innumerable contributions to the musical identity of Nashville, The Station Inn is a space in crisis. As the high rises climb ever higher and as urban pioneers descend, frequenting hip pubs and high-end restaurants, The Station Inn rebels and rebukes the modern through its insistence on and performance of its decidedly un-gentrified charm.

After over forty years in business, The Station Inn faces perhaps its greatest threat yet with the increasingly encroaching Gulch project entering yet another expansive phase. Current owner J. T. Gray rents the building that houses The Station Inn, and a recent 2014 report on Nashville Public Radio revealed that the quarter-acre beneath the building is worth nearly half a million dollars.[10] Despite MarketStreet's insistence that it is "a wonderful amenity to have in the neighborhood, and something you just can't re-create," and their promise to "build around" it and not "do anything with the building as long as [Gray] runs the club," the writing appears on the freshly poured concrete wall.[11] In late February another iconic Nashville music venue, 12th and Porter, closed its doors, victim of an eerily similar gentrification project, complete with high rise condos, retail, and restaurants, in the so-called "North Gulch" redevelopment area.[12] While it is now too late for 12th and Porter and its rock 'n' roll clientele, the stages of these threatened music venues offer vibrant potential performance spaces that directly and indirectly address the turf war occurring throughout Nashville. Enter The Station Inn's Doyle and Debbie.

Onto The Station Inn stage, one night a week, every week, in the heart of the contested space of The Gulch, enters *The Doyle and Debbie Show*, a parody, written and first performed in 2006, that "simultaneously lampoons and idolizes country music's tradition of iconic duets and their subsequent battle of the sexes."[13] Actors Bruce Arntson and Jenny Littleton embody the fictional musical duo of Doyle and Debbie, a struggling country act trying to claw its way back to the heights of country radio after Doyle's public meltdown. Theirs is a metatheatrical performance, using the authentic space of The Station Inn as a backdrop for their fictional concert. They walk a delicate tightrope between irony (poking fun at country music convention) and reverence (paying homage to past artists). Their musical numbers, which include ditties like "Whine Whine, Twang Twang," "Barefoot and Pregnant," and "For the Children," poke fun at country music, "rural," and southern stereotypes of gender and class while simultaneously relying heavily on those same country music conventions to generate humor (see figure 6).[14]

The Doyle and Debbie Show plays with space on at least two primary levels: within their chosen performative space of parody and within the

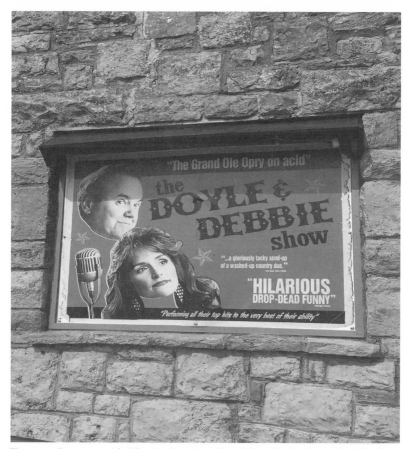

Figure 6. Poster outside The Station Inn advertising *The Doyle and Debbie Show*. Nashville, Tennessee. Courtesy of Chase Bringardner.

physical space of The Station Inn and its location in The Gulch. The space of parody exists within the show at both a literal and figurative level. Literally, the performance adopts the guise and structure of parody through the physical placement of the actors appearing in costume and makeup as fictional characters juxtaposed within the authentic physical space of the historic stage of The Station Inn. Figuratively, the performance creates an imagined or conjured parodic space that exists between the representation and the referent, between Doyle and Debbie and the country acts and tropes they parody. At every level, the show constructs a liminal performance offering up Doyle and Debbie as an interspatial threshold between the past and the present, the old and the new, The Station Inn and The Gulch. Through their performance, Doyle and Debbie create a space that argues for the preservation of the past (or at least some of it) against the pressing forces of the modern and sounds a clarion call linking the survival of The Station Inn to a victory over The Gulch and other gentrifying threats.

Both Arntson and Littleton bring to *The Doyle and Debbie Show* a level of country music authenticity necessary for their parodic performance. Arntson spent nearly forty years in Nashville surrounded by the inner workings of the country music industry before he began writing *The Doyle and Debbie Show*. As a musician and performer, he brought to the creative process a deep knowledge of the various facets of the country music form and a real appreciation for musicianship. His position within the music community afforded him a certain position of authority and gifted him the respect of the very community he parodies in the show. As he states, "A lot of people have done bad country music parody (because it is like shooting fish in a barrel), but when Jenny and I did it we were pretty well versed in that old-school country music, so we treat it with respect. The idea was to have satire combined with homage; hopefully, in Nashville, that [approach] would tickle people rather than piss them off."[15] While she does not possess the same insider status, Littleton, who portrays Debbie, likewise is well versed in the country music tradition. Her skill at mimicking female country singers like Dolly Parton and Patsy Cline provides Arntson's song parodies an additional layer of authenticity.

Arntson created *The Doyle and Debbie Show* while working on a biography program for Country Music Television. While pulling together archival footage, Arntson stumbled upon syndicated shows of the 1960s and 1970s like *The Porter Wagoner Show* and *Pop Goes the Country*, wherein "those old-time [stars]" would "do their impression of show business and it'd have an awkward yet charming approach, like 'hillbilly vaudeville.'"[16] Arntson found inspiration within this forgotten form of entertainment and saw within it the potential to repurpose and revive such performance for a modern audience: "It was begging for someone to parody it."[17] He strongly embraced the performance for the way it relishes the juxtaposition of the "endearingly amateur" and a "weird professional sheen."[18] For Arntson, this combination made the form perfect for capturing the tensions running through the history of country music and more specifically the struggle for modern audiences to reconcile with country music's often colorful past, rife with overt sexism, racism, and stereotype.

Arntson's use of parody as his chosen performative strategy allows him to position himself in the space between reverence and comedy, balancing confidently yet precariously in the middle, operating inside while simultaneously commenting from the outside. Parody, as Linda Hutcheon reminds in *A Theory of Parody*, "is a complex genre, in terms of both its form and its ethos. It is one of the ways in which modern artists have managed to come to terms with the weight of the past."[19] In *The Doyle and Debbie Show*, Arntson and Littleton fervently embody the past, complete with big hair and fringe-trimmed jackets, investing completely in the characters and their perceived reality as a touring musical act straight out of those shows Arntson saw in the archives. As Jewly Hight states in her 2015 piece on the show in *Nashville Scene*: "Doyle and Debbie keep the over-the-top musical references to '50s, '60s and '70s country coming, even as they artfully gesture toward retrograde performing dynamics (a male singer with a wounded ego, who constantly belittles his fetching younger, greener female partner) beneath their down-home, vaudevillian patter. With this show, the parody works both ways; they send up country entertainers' habit of repurposing age-old shtick and letting audiences feel like they're in on the jokes, just as they send up the tradition of country outsiders dismissing the genre wholesale with shallow, class-based stereotypes."[20] The humor, and in turn the meaning of the piece, comes from a series of juxtapositions; the juxtaposition of their authentic commitment to their material with the sheen of their performance of that material; the juxtaposition of the embodiment of historical stereotype with a modern sensibility of what is considered retrograde; the juxtaposition of being inside the joke and being outside the genre. Theorist Susan Stewart has described parody as the act of "substituting elements within a dimension of a given text in such a way that the resulting text stands in an inverse or incongruous relation to the borrowed text."[21] The content of the dialogue and lyrics that pushes the various issues (sexism, racism, stereotypes, etc.) to the forefront in a knowing, excessive, and deliberate way stands in "an inverse or incongruous relation" to the very form of the carefully constructed country music duo itself.[22] As a parodic performance, *The Doyle and Debbie Show* within its own structure engages with spatial concerns, positioning the act of performance as a space for simultaneous gesturing backward and forward, toward the past and the modern.

The Doyle and Debbie Show couches this simultaneous gesturing forward and backward, often made evident or visible in parody through the proverbial wink, within the larger structure of a somewhat traditional theatre piece. Even though Arntson mentions Vaudeville as one of his chief influences, he contends that "obviously it is a theater piece, a 90-minute musical comedy."[23] He adamantly "didn't want just a jukebox-musical"; he wanted a dramatic arc.[24] This insistence results in the overall premise of the show: Doyle and Debbie embark on a comeback tour after some initially unexplained incident that left Doyle in treatment and swearing off alcohol. The song "Daddy's Hair" marks the theatrical climax, wherein Doyle, after secretly consuming alcohol throughout the first two-thirds of the show, experiences a psychotic break onstage, in response to drunkenly viewing and then wearing his father's scalp (yes, scalp) that he has removed from a tin box he carries around with him. Debbie's reentrance onstage reestablishes order and leads to the resolution.

Littleton's performance as Debbie #3 (a recent replacement for Debbie #2) provides a clear example of how the performance embraces and embodies the precarious, often hilarious parodic space in between sincerity and mockery, the past and the present, within their theatrical structure. Her performance borrows heavily from the well-trod trope of the struggling single mother trying to make a better life for herself and her children. At one point in the performance, Littleton as Debbie even has to exit the space and go into the actual parking lot to break up a fight between her kids who are waiting in the station wagon. Her characterization of Debbie reflects the biographies of the women whose style she parodies. Yet in her ability to slide seamlessly between the specific vocal stylings of Dolly, Loretta, and Patsy (to name a few), she demonstrates an aptitude and skill level that rises well above the confines of her character. Likewise, her vocal prowess stands in firm opposition to her subservient, blatantly sexist victim Debbie within the act wherein Doyle belittles and undermines her at every turn. "Barefoot and Pregnant," one of her earliest numbers, illustrates Littleton's strategy. Littleton confidently attacks the song with a vocal style harkening back to the Dolly Parton from the days of *The Porter Wagoner Show* while fiercely committing to the overtly sexist content as Debbie. Her commitment to the sexist material in juxtaposition with her profound technical skill performed alongside Arntson's overtly sexist Doyle sells the parody; as Arntson remarks, "If the balance is done right, then it's funny and not annoying. If the balance isn't right, then the show looks sexist."[25]

In addition to gender, *The Doyle and Debbie Show* expands the literal and figurative parodic space to comment upon other issues as well. Toward the end of the show, Doyle and Debbie perform a medley of their supposed "other" hits, concluding with the song "God Loves America Best." While previous songs have almost exclusively parodied classic country music, only occasionally venturing as far as the 1980s, "God Loves America Best" decidedly takes its parodic aim at the rah-rah patriotism of post-9/11 country music, and especially the work of Toby Keith. Keith famously proclaimed in his 2002 song "Courtesy of the Red, White, and Blue (The Angry American)":

> And you'll be sorry that you messed with
> The US of A.
> 'Cause we'll put a boot in your ass
> It's the American way.[26]

Arntson and Littleton intentionally channel and parody Keith and his contemporaries' patriotic extremism. Through parodying such a contemporary song alongside older ones, *The Doyle and Debbie Show* makes an argument for the continued presence of retrograde, regressive ideas in country music, drawing parallels between the sexism of the 1950s and 1960s with the jingoism found in some contemporary country music. This song illustrates the continued ability of parody to create a space for playful critique that gestures to the modern and allows the audience to participate, or be in on the joke.

Yet this parodic space cannot exist without a physical space that supports and encourages such performance. The particular venue of The Station Inn allows *The Doyle and Debbie Show* to get away with the parody. Performing in a space steeped in country music history gives the show the authenticity that allows even musicians like Keith to respect Arntson and Littleton as fellow artists with just enough reverence for country music to not cross into mockery.[27] Doyle and Debbie, the characters, perform their show in the actual Station Inn as if they were any other touring musical act. As a result, the audience is always in the actual Station Inn as opposed to a created, theatrical environment. For example, when Debbie leaves to attend to her children, she exits through the actual front door, the door the audience entered through, presumably going to the same parking lot where audience members parked their own cars. This moment cements the rootedness and specificity of the physical space, reminding the audience of the convention that Doyle and Debbie are performing in The Station Inn itself and not a theatrical venue.

Just as Doyle and Debbie strategically use the stage of The Station Inn to claw their way back to success, the performance itself configures the audience as actively working, through their presence, for the survival of the venue itself. The physical space of The Station Inn is always already seen in relation to The Gulch, both in geographical reality and in the performance (see figure 7). As a result, when we root for Doyle and Debbie's successful return despite their old-fashioned charm, we actively root against the villainous forces of modernity embodied by the encroaching gentrifying presence of ever-rising condo buildings, trendy restaurants, and abundant retail spaces that clearly frame and overwhelm the performance space within The Gulch itself.

The Doyle and Debbie Show struggled at first with trying to determine its own spatial relationship to its audience. Initially the show was performed in the Bongo Theater Upstairs, a small, intimate black box theatre above a coffee house. Yet the more overtly theatrical space worked against the nature of the piece, emphasizing the theatricality and undercutting the piece's precarious relationship with authenticity. The Station Inn gives

Figure 7. The Station Inn in the shadow of the Gulch development project. Nashville, Tennessee. Courtesy of Chase Bringardner.

the performance a certain spatial legitimacy; the genuine bluegrass venue authenticates their act, adding weight and legitimacy to their portrayal of a country duo while allowing the audience a more solid, less theatrical foundation that heightens the juxtaposition and thus the humor.[28]

The spatial dynamics of the venue also determine the composition of the audience. Audiences in the black box space tended toward a more Nashville theatre crowd or hipster coffee house crowd, whereas The Station Inn attracts a strikingly different clientele. The audience on any given night, according to Arntson, comprises two distinct groups: "In general, we get baby boomers . . . maybe they didn't necessarily listen to George Jones and Porter Wagoner, but they have the context and can appreciate the music. These are really salacious and sexist songs that we're being ironic about to make a point. They get that. But then, we do get a type of hard-core-country fan who doesn't seem to need the irony to appreciate the show. 'Fat Women in Trailers' to them is really about fat women in trailers. There's no irony involved."[29] The musical venue allows both of these segments of audience to coexist within the same space while the form of parody invites, in this instance, a variety of possible reception strategies. Thus the relationship between The Station Inn and *The Doyle and Debbie Show* is a symbiotic one. The performance of *The Doyle and Debbie Show* at The Station Inn emphasizes and underscores the legitimacy of The Station Inn as a truly important, historical bluegrass venue while simultaneously locating the venue as modern through its embrace of a parody that makes fun of the past. At the same time the space of The Station Inn legitimizes *The Doyle and Debbie Show* as firmly rooted in country music tradition, offering a firm foundation and context for their parody while also acknowledging the authentic musicianship of the performers. As Jewly Hight stated in her piece for the *Nashville Scene*, the show "wouldn't work at all, and certainly not at a bastion of bluegrass authenticity like The Station Inn . . . if the music lacked a certain degree of knowledge, skill and affectionate attention to detail."[30] Even the most discerning audience member, well versed in the nuances of country music, can appreciate the humor, in part because of the stamp of authenticity and approval the space of The Station Inn provides.

One particularly significant fan of the show is Station Inn owner J. T. Gray who, according to Arntson, "likes it because we're musically knowing."[31] Arntson and Littleton's extensive musical knowledge befits the stature of Gray's historic venue. Moreover, Gray enjoys the fact that the show appeals to a wide audience, simultaneously attracting musicians, songwriters, country music fans, people who do not like the genre, and Nashville's burgeoning tourist industry. The broad parodic gestures of *The Doyle and Debbie Show* create an inclusive, welcoming audience space wherein people can identify with multiple levels of performance simultaneously. They can laugh knowing they are a part of the humor, both inside and outside of the joke at any given moment.

Moreover, the theatrical interplay between *The Doyle and Debbie Show* and the space of The Station Inn itself reveals a larger activist spatial performance, unveiling and highlighting the complex layers of space at play in the larger neighborhood: Nashville . . . The Gulch . . . The Station Inn . . . *The Doyle and Debbie Show*. Doyle and Debbie perform an ironic nostalgia that comments on the changing place of country music in a more modern society. The anxieties expressed in the show mirror the anxieties of the space surrounded by the gentrifying forces of The Gulch and Nashville. In other words, for The Station Inn, the space, just like Doyle and Debbie, must play into and play up its nostalgic, bluegrass/country past in order to stave off the forces of modernization. Doyle and Debbie perform a spatial parody and politics that argues for the survival of The Station Inn through a careful interplay of convention and irony that seeks to carve out and stake a place within the changing, re-gentrified landscape.

Notes

1. "The Development," *The Gulch: Get Down Here*, accessed April 6, 2015, http://www.nashvillegulch.com/index.php/about.

2. Ibid.

3. Ibid.

4. Ibid.

5. Ibid.

6. Ibid.

7. Chas Sisk, "Nashville's Iconic Station Inn Hangs On for Now in Transformed Gulch," *Nashville Public Radio*, December 19, 2014, http://nashvillepublicradio.org/post/nashville-s-iconic-station-inn-hangs-now-transformed-gulch-neighborhood.

8. "History," *The Station Inn*, accessed April 1, 2015, http://stationinn.com/index01/about-us/.

9. The plastic sign found outside The Station Inn is purported to be the original sign from the 1978 relocation. While visual evidence seems to support that assertion, whether it is true remains undocumented in the history section of the venue's website.

10. Sisk, "Nashville's Iconic Station Inn Hangs On for Now in Transformed Gulch."

11. "The Development."

12. Zach Blumfenfeld, "Gentrification Is Taking the Music Out of Music City,"

WRVU Nashville, February 5, 2015, http://wrvu.org/gentrification-is-taking-the-music-out-of-music-city/.

13. *The Doyle and Debbie Show*, accessed April 1, 2015, http://www.doyleanddebbie.com/.

14. Ibid.

15. Basil Consindine, "Behind 'The Doyle & Debbie Show': Interview with Composer-Playwright Bruce Arntson," *Twin Cities Dailey Planet*, March 23, 2014, http://www.tcdailyplanet.net/interview-bruce-arntson-behind-doyle-debbie-show/.

16. Ibid.

17. Ibid.

18. Laura Molzahn, "Getting to Know Bruce Arntson, One Half of 'The Doyle & Debbie Show,'" *WBEZ-91.5*, November 16, 2011, http://www.wbez.org/blog/onstagebackstage/2011–11–16/getting-know-bruce-arntson-one-half-doyle-debbie-show-94092.

19. Linda Hutcheon, *A Theory of Parody: The Teachings of Twentieth-Century Art Forms* (New York: Methuen, 1985), 29.

20. Jewly Hight, "Longtime Music City Satirists Doyle and Debbie Return to the Station Inn," *Nashville Scene*, July 3, 2014, http://www.nashvillescene.com/nashville/longtime-music-city-satirists-doyle-and-debbie-return-to-the-station-inn/Content?oid=4223781.

21. Susan Stewart, quoted in Hutcheon, *A Theory of Parody*, 36.

22. Ibid.

23. Hight, "Longtime Music City Satirists Doyle and Debbie Return to the Station Inn."

24. Molzahn, "Getting to Know Bruce Arntson, One Half of 'The Doyle & Debbie Show.'"

25. Consindine, "Behind 'The Doyle & Debbie Show': Interview with Composer-Playwright Bruce Arntson."

26. Toby Keith, "Courtesy of the Red, White, and Blue," accessed April 1, 2015, http://www.azlyrics.com/lyrics/tobykeith/ courtesyoftheredwhiteandbluetheangryamerican.html.

27. Toby Keith has expressed his respect for the show. As Arntson notes in an interview with Michael Dukes, "Bruce's Big Adventure: *The Doyle and Debbie Show* Gets Ready for Hollywood Baby!," *Nashville Arts*, August 31, 2014, http://nashvillearts.com/2014/08/29/bruces-big-adventure: "Toby Keith has embraced us. He flew us to his country club and had us do the show at his Christmas party. And there we are, doing songs like 'God Loves America Best.' After the show, Toby's manager told me he turned to Toby during that one and asked, you think they're making fun of you? Toby nodded, but he was laughing. He loved it. He gets what we're doing."

28. Michael Dukes, "Bruce's Big Adventure: *The Doyle and Debbie Show* Gets Ready for Hollywood Baby!," *Nashville Arts*, August 31, 2014, http://nashvillearts.com/2014/08/29/bruces-big-adventure/.

29. Ibid.

30. Hight, "Longtime Music City Satirists Doyle and Debbie Return to the Station Inn."

31. Ibid.

(Un)limited

Virtual Performance Spaces and Digital Identity

Alicia Corts

Many new online performance spaces surround us in the digital age. From social media platforms like Facebook and Snapchat, to anonymous social media tools like Yik Yak, to graphic social media environments like Second Life, virtual performance gives users the opportunity to create identities that go well beyond what was previously possible. John McCarthy and Peter Wright suggest that when we encounter technology, the space of that interaction changes the concrete, visceral reactions each user experiences as well as the actions and emotions within the space.[1] In other words, by entering new virtual spaces of performance, we experience ways of performing that step outside the boundaries of the physical world, giving the illusion that virtual performance is unlimited. For example, Julian Dibbell describes "tripping with compulsive regularity down the well-traveled information lane" where he "checks [his] quotidian identity, steps into the persona and appearance" of another character altogether and, if the mood strikes him, "emerges as a dolphin instead."[2]

While researchers like Dibbell have focused on the freedom of identity play in virtual spaces, I am interested in how the virtual performance space itself influences the ways in which users create virtual identities, specifically in social media outlets like Yik Yak and graphic virtual worlds like Second Life. In the physical world, identity grows out of interacting with objects and people, then reflecting on those interactions.[3] In virtual spaces, designers have programmed the system that allows users to interact and communicate with objects and people. With the proliferation of virtual spaces, it is important to examine these hidden boundaries to understand who and what shape identity creation. Game users enter virtual spaces of performance unaware of the ways in which the limitations of the program influence their performances and, through reflection on that performance, the identity-creation process. While users adapt to virtual performance spaces, they often remain unaware of how programs directly and indirectly influence their choices, and in turn influence the creation of online cultural norms.

Users of virtual spaces reshape or completely transform their physical world identities. Commenting on the performance of identity, Erving Goffman asserts that the presentation of self is reliant on the sign system present at the site of the performance.[4] Each virtual space relies on a different sign system to present that self. In Julian Dibbell's case, the space accommodates a performance free from the confines of the physical body, allowing him to present himself as a dolphin. Users of Facebook, on the other hand, craft an online identity through the careful curation of photos and specific status updates, but the identity does not necessarily match the reality of life behind the screen.[5] The programming behind each digital platform dictates the sign system, limiting how communication can flow between participants. The Facebook page hosts pictures of the user, while a graphic virtual world, like the one Dibbell references, relies on images that have nothing to do with his actual physical appearance. His presentation of self, in Goffman's terms, is limited by the program.

Two dominant theories have emerged in sociology surrounding identity creation: reflexivity and habitus.[6] Reflexivity refers to identity creation that results from activities or interactions that force a person to "bend back," or refer to themselves during an interaction, affecting the formation of identity.[7] As an example, a teacher returns a humorous essay assignment to a student. The student, following the directions, used a story well known in his family about a moment when the family car nearly ran over a dog in the road, something the student's family tells with great laughter every time. The teacher expresses horror at the humorous tone in the essay, and with the feedback, the student can "bend back" and reflect on both the choice of the story and whether that story is something that he should continue to tell outside his family. More deeply, the student may reflect on whether his family's sense of humor labels his taste in humor as inappropriate to others in society.

Whereas reflexivity is about self-awareness brought on after an action, habitus revolves around the boundaries society sets on performance. Bourdieu coined the term habitus for the process a society uses to define the parameters of behavior monitored through an invisible system of expectations, behaviors, and tastes.[8] When the teacher expresses discomfort over the student's story, she is guiding the student away from a subject that this particular society does not consider to be humorous: the near-death of an animal. The teacher's actions demonstrate how habitus works. Rather than having a written set of rules about what is appropriate for a humorous essay, the teacher instead expresses concern over a topic that does not fit society's expectations. Both theories—reflexivity and habitus—point to the importance of interacting with the world in order to form identity; most sociologists believe that a combination of the two theories provides a complete understanding of identity creation.[9] In the case of performing in virtual spaces, each theory opens up a conversation regarding how the space itself can mold the identity of the user.

To demonstrate how virtual space influences identity creation, I analyze two distinctly different virtual spaces, Yik Yak and Second Life, and the ways they potentially mold user identity, both directly and indirectly. In each case, a user enters into the space with the freedom to create a new identity unconnected to their physical world identity. Each of the two spaces has specific program designs that directly limit the interactions users can have. These same limits shape the cultural norms of each virtual performance space. The space, therefore, alters the presentation of self, limiting identity creation within these virtual spaces.

Yik Yak: Identity Creation through Anonymous Posts

Yik Yak is "an anonymous messaging app that allows users to create and view posts—called Yaks—within a 10 mile radius."[10] It is truly anonymous to the casual user: there are no usernames or other identifying information associated with each comment.[11] Not only are the comments completely anonymous, but each post also disappears from the feed no longer than forty-eight hours after posting. Started in 2013, this app has quickly become popular on college campuses as a way of transmitting information and commenting on life events.

When a user logs into Yik Yak, they see a very simple interface. They can either post a new yak or read what other people have to say. The user has the ability to vote on yaks, which is the critical element to this virtual performance space. Upvotes win the poster "yakarma," a reward system unique in that there are no rewards. Points are accumulated but are not worth any material goods. Yakarma can be thought of as quantified bragging rights rather than any sort of prize after a competition. A user earns points for anonymous posts and voting on other posts, but there is no way for an individual to brag about a post to others with any reliability. Yakarma is solely a reward for acceptable activity in the space, a "cultural validation" for posts that meet community standards.[12] In addition, yaks with the most upvotes are awarded the "famous" badge and placed on a special "hot" list, rewarding the original poster with even more yakarma. Users are, therefore, encouraged to post popular yaks to gain yakarma points. The space is set up to reward yakkers with the best posts, since upvotes gain the most yakarma. Yaks can completely disappear if they receive four or more downvotes. In other words, if a user is not interesting or offends the group, their yak will disappear.[13]

Consider these recent yaks. The following three yaks represent a single second on the University of Georgia's Yik Yak space:

> 1. If you crowd around the doors of the bus at the Tate stop when I'm trying to get off, I will push you out of the way. (no replies, one minute after posting, zero votes)
> 2. Chaco shoes smelling bad now with the sweat and only worn then [*sic*] twice...tips for smell? (three replies, two minutes after posting, zero votes)
> 3. Still giving out free t-shirts at Memorial? (three replies, two minutes, four upvotes)[14]

Assume that three different people posted these statements. One is a grumpy warning about pushy people at the bus stop, a response to what was, no doubt, a rough afternoon at one of the most crowded bus stops on campus. If the goal of the space is to gain yakarma, this poster assumes that their yak will speak to others in a similar position. Truly popular yaks at UGA begin receiving votes within seconds. This yak about the Tate bus stop had a score of 0 votes, meaning either no one voted on it or the negative and positive votes balanced each other out. Regardless, when the original poster looks at the response to this yak, the process of reflexivity begins. The original poster sent the yak into the community as a way to interact with the larger group, but the community did not respond positively. Assuming the poster is committed to performing in the Yik Yak space, the poster has to look at the opinion expressed in the yak and rethink why the community rejected their attempt at fitting in. Even if a person is not self-aware enough to wish to fit into the community, yakarma becomes a way of rewarding those who do make the effort to follow the community's standards. Yakarma comes to those who best model the community's standards and can convince people to upvote. When the original poster "bends back" on their performance,[15] they can see that in order to fit into the community, something has to change: Was the suggestion of violence too much? Is the Tate bus stop uninteresting? Regardless, the original poster is left to reflect on how the expressed opinion fell short of piquing community interest, and the space sets that yakker up to reflexively consider identity within the confines of the University of Georgia.

Yik Yak is also a wonderful example of how habitus is set up in virtual space. Habitus is the set of unwritten rules that govern habits, behaviors, tastes, and expectations, and this social media application acts like a virtual courtroom, judging whether opinions fit in with a particular community. By yakking, a person is asking for community support of an opinion. Habitus is transmitted by cultural commentary on behaviors and opinions as they are expressed. As Bourdieu notes, children are rebuked or redirected when they step outside community norms, and those rebukes not only build habitus but also establish a pattern for how to further enforce community rules in adulthood.[16] When a new virtual community forms within Yik Yak, it begins to enforce new cultural rules with other users, similar to the way in which children are indoctrinated into society in the physical world. In the virtual space, new norms are established by the simple framework of the space: yakarma is the goal and upvotes are the way of demonstrating what the community, at large, approves or disapproves of.

One way to identify the habitus of a Yik Yak space is through the "hot list," a set of yaks with the most votes over the previous twenty-four hours. Following are three yaks from the hot list captured at the same time as the previous three yaks:

> 1. Do you ever create a fake scenario in your head and get so caught up in it that you have to be like, "wait, it's not even real, why am i so angry right now." (nine replies, two hours since posting, one hundred upvotes)
> 2. April is GPA awareness month. (no replies, two hours since posting, seventy-seven upvotes)
> 3. It always makes me smile when the food service employees interact with us [students]. It might not be the best job, but they make the most of it by trying to make us smile. So many amazing people here. (thirteen replies, three hours since posting, seventy-one upvotes)[17]

Looking at this list, we can see what Rotenberg and McDonough refer to as a "sense of place," the collection of meanings society has associated with a particular space and the activities within that space.[18] In their anthropological research, Rotenberg and McDonough look at how urban spaces develop specific cultural meaning and boundaries; their assertion that spaces hold specific cultural rules and values can be seen in how Yik Yak works as a specific, virtual space on the University of Georgia campus. The above Yik Yak hotlist can only be accessed by those users in close spatial proximity to the campus, so what we see in this short list is an example of what the Yik Yak community at the University of Georgia values. First, the GPA post shows not only an awareness of the activity driving the university, but it reflects the community norm that clever, original humor should be rewarded. While this post might not be the first time that anyone has stated that April is GPA awareness month, it was the first time that it had been posted at UGA.[19] Once a yak has been seen by the community, however, continual reposting of the same yak results in immediate downvoting. To test this theory, I reposted the same yak a day later: it was downvoted in less than two minutes. In addition to clever humor, Yik Yak at UGA rewards two other kinds of yaks: the introspective and the kind. The first yak on this list demonstrates both humor and introspection, while the third yak shows kindness toward a revered group of people, the food service employees at UGA.

As a performance space, Yik Yak affects identity through habitus by creating a complex collection of community rules that control and outline what is proper and improper behavior and opinion. Yik Yak has become known as a place where offensive behaviors proliferate,[20] but it is important to recognize how a specific community responds to improper yaks. A colleague, for example, reposted an offensive yak on her Facebook wall, pointing to the yak as an example of how racism is still alive and well at UGA. The yak read, "Most of the dead students were minorities. Good riddance. You don't belong at UGA, even God agrees [one reply stating, "That's fucked up," thirty-nine seconds after posting, four downvotes]."[21] Here, the poster is referring to the annual UGA memorial service where community members who have died are honored and remembered. As you can see, the original poster put out the opinion that God hates minorities. The comment is deeply offensive, but consider the way the UGA Yik Yak space discourages this performance and the identity implied by it: Within thirty-nine seconds, this yak has been voted off. The −4 rating shows that it is about to disappear; the person who captured this screenshot and posted it to Facebook saved the performance just in time. In addition, there was a person who saw this yak within seconds of it going live in the Yik Yak space and commented negatively on it. In this case, the original poster would receive notification that there was a comment and the yak had been offvoted.

The UGA Yik Yak community could have ignored this poster, but instead yakkers responded within seconds to say that this poster's opinion had no place at UGA. There are overt rules against racism on UGA's campus, but in this virtual performance space, the unwritten rules of habitus indicate that it is in bad taste to post offensive remarks about minorities. When the original poster revisits the comment and begins the process of reflexively using the feedback for identity building, they will have to consider whether maintaining racist views is worth such swift downvoting by the Yik Yak community, and whether building an online identity within this space is beneficial. The UGA Yik Yak platform will not reward this particular identity. A small amount of yakarma will be rewarded to the poster just for posting the original yak, but because the yak was so quickly downvoted, they will not receive the more substantial yakarma reward built into the space.

In this way, Yik Yak restricts users directly by guiding their interactions (voting and posting). It also indirectly works to shape the expectations and tastes of the community. The program itself creates boundaries that prohibit certain performances, thereby limiting reflexivity and community response to an individual as they work toward identity creation. If Yik Yak as a space did not promote yakarma as the goal for users, then users would not feel compelled to upvote and downvote yaks and create the communal performance boundaries for (in)appropriate behavior.

For a space to be capable of limiting performance, Thomas Gieryn asserts that it requires three elements: a unique, identifiable spot in the universe, objects within the space that must be interacted with, and investment of meaning and value within the space.[22] Virtual spaces may seem counterintuitive as performance spaces, since there is no materiality. An online performance is only pixels and text. Yet virtual spaces like Yik Yak possess the three qualities necessary to control performance, and, in creating those boundaries, virtual spaces regulate and guide identity creation.

In contrast to the Yik Yak virtual space, in the next example I want to explore specifically how the programming of objects within a space can create performance boundaries. Whereas Yik Yak is a virtual performance space that uses text as a means of performance, Second Life uses both graphics and text. Objects that users interact with, therefore, become more important since Second Life users choose virtual bodies and move through the virtual world to create identities.

Second Life: Space as Invisible Boundary

Second Life is a virtual world started in 2002 that has several thousand users, known as residents, online at any given moment. While similar in appearance to games such as World of Warcraft, Second Life has no rules or goals for users to achieve, making it a more specialized graphic social media platform rather than a game. Second Life residents make friends, send messages, and interact much as Facebook users would. The difference is that instead of using their physical world identities, Second Life residents choose an animated mesh body with a new name unconnected to the physical world.[23] Cory Ondrejka, one of the original Linden Lab developers responsible for creating the world, calls Second Life a place where users "create iteratively and interactively" to develop content and "a strong and diverse social network."[24] This world relies on its users as the primary developers of content, with over ninety percent of its virtual world created by residents. Each area of Second Life has distinct architecture. From a replica of the Eiffel Tower to shopping districts more extensive than the largest physical-world malls to elaborate botanical gardens, there are a variety of places in which to perform. Each sim, or digital land area, in Second Life is unique and identifiable: a clothing store looks and functions differently from a concert venue, for example.[25]

When a resident walks into a clothing store, they might see clothing racks, chairs, and a selection of clothing that can be worn on the animated mesh avatar body. As mentioned, each object is crafted by residents themselves, and the objects are given value based on how well they are made and the objects' importance within the community.[26] Visualize a barstool. Such an object is easy to craft, and many residents who learn to craft objects in Second Life start with this project. It takes great skill, therefore, to take a common object and make it extraordinary, just as it would in the physical world. Anyone can make a rather ugly and wobbly barstool, but it takes skill to create one that individual users will want to display inside Second Life.

Residents in Second Life do not display all of the objects they have purchased or created. Rather, they carefully choose which bar stool to display in their clubs. A new user might pick a simple bar stool that looks like a cushion stuck on the end of a pin. A more savvy user will choose a bar stool with a seat back, a cushion textured to look like velvet, and a shiny, metal base. When a user interacts with objects—such as a bar stool in a Second Life pub—the interface within the virtual space provides approval similar to the upvoting and downvoting in Yik Yak, though more subtly and over a greater span of time. For example, if I started a bar in Second Life and chose to display a cheap bar stool, I would feel the community's disapproval by how many other residents spent time in my establishment. The objects themselves are just pixels, but how I am treated by others in the community when I choose one object over another shows the object's value. Subsequently, the objects found in Second Life have gained the seal of approval from residents because they have chosen to allow others to see and, in the case of a barstool, use the object by sitting on and interacting with it. Each digital object is filled with potential and meaning by the community, which has invested in it. Bourdieu calls these types of objects "objectivated cultural capital," objects that hold society's approval or disapproval.[27] By displaying certain objects over others, residents indicate what they prefer and imbue with meaning.

The avatar body is one such locus of objectivated cultural capital. The user crafts his Second Life body carefully, choosing a body shape and skin.[28] Since other Second Life users cannot connect the user's avatar to the physical world identity of the user, gender play is a common practice for both male and female users.[29] In Second Life human avatar bodies are coded to demonstrate the gender biology characteristics of male and female; in order to engage in gender play, participants must choose avatars of the opposite sex. Because the visual symbols of physical-world biological sex becomes the visual sign for gender in Second Life, the program's privileging of human bodies also privileges traditionally "gendered" bodies.[30] In this sense, gender play is regulated by the space itself. While it appears as if the user may choose their avatar body based on personal preference, the space exerts a powerful influence on which bodies move most easily through Second Life. Second Life starter avatars were, until recently, only available in human, "gendered" form, requiring the new user to choose a male or female body to enter the virtual world.[31] This regulation within the platform from its beginning in 2003 has made "gendered" performance the norm.

In contrast to "gendered" human bodies, when residents choose nonhuman avatar bodies, objects become particularly important. Seemingly nonhuman bodies are possible in Second Life, but the space makes it difficult to perform such bodies seamlessly in the environment. Take, for example, the simple act of sitting. When a resident using a human avatar sits in a chair, that resident activates an animation that moves the avatar body into a human sitting position. The chair either uses a standard animation that can be activated by either traditionally male or female avatars or gives the resident interacting with the object the choice of male and female animation.[32] Returning to Bordieu's terminology, the resident has used two "objectivated cultural objects" in that moment: the human-shaped avatar body and the chair using human animations. Rather than simply being a chair, this object holds the cultural values associated with the animations included in the chair. By reading this object, we can see which bodies the virtual community values. Since human—or male and female—animations are included in chairs, these bodies become the privileged ones within this virtual performance space. When I choose to sit on the chair, my avatar mesh body sits in a human, female position. Because I have chosen the body that the program suggested for me when I first signed up (female, human body), my experience in Second Life is smooth and uninterrupted with animations that do not fit my body. The culture of Second Life ultimately came to privilege "gendered," human body types because the program sets them up as the starter avatar bodies. In Second Life, residents can choose to perform as "non-gendered" avatars (animals, fantasy characters, or inanimate objects), but these performances stand out because the bodies remain Other when seen in the context of the community as a whole. In other words, the virtual space pushes individual residents—and thereby the virtual community—to privilege human bodies over all other choices residents can make. Human animations are standard in all chairs. In fact, most chairs have animations for two types of human bodies: male and female. Since residents interact with this type of furniture all the time, they become used to seeing human (and by association, traditionally "gendered") bodies using furniture.

To illustrate this point, consider what happens when the avatar changes to a hippo, one of the many nonhuman bodies available in Second Life, and sits in the same chair. Animal avatars take on an otherworldly, cartoonish quality in this virtual world, and the gender of the user cannot be determined from their bodies. When nonhuman bodies are subjected to the same animations as the more common human avatar body and its associated male or female animation, the animal body looks ridiculous and out of place. For example, in the case of the hippo, the animal's hind quarters protrude out of the back of the chair, the front legs bend at an odd angle underneath the animal, and the head sticks out of the seat. The impression this type of avatar gives any casual observer is that the hippo ran into the chair, accidentally getting it stuck around its neck. Chairs are found everywhere in Second Life, and since the space requires animations to manipulate the avatar body, builders put animations into each object so that the most common type of body can use the furniture with ease. Hippo furniture is possible in Second Life, and a builder could easily create the item. But such objects do not exist commonly because the standard of the program is the coding of an image that mimics the gender binary of human male and female.

In fact, the hippo may appear on the surface to be an animal, but the human, "gendered" avatar body still lurks beneath the surface. In order to create the illusion of the hippo body, various pieces of the hippo have to be attached to the human avatar mesh, which is bent backward into something resembling a bridge pose in yoga. At the same time, the body is stretched to a skeletal thinness. Various parts of the hippo are then attached to the human avatar body, such as the front legs to the human avatar's arms. While the human avatar body is deformed, it is still the basis for the hippo body. Animations manipulate the human body and not the attachments, creating the illusion of a hippo, so that when an animation is activated, the stretched and deformed human body responds. If a sitting animation moves the human legs into a crossed-leg position, the stiff hippo legs move based on the human underneath. The human body underneath, however, does not correlate to the orientation of the hippo. The human mesh form underneath is pointed toward the sky while the hippo is pointing downward. If a chair indicates a human should sit forward, the hippo will face in the opposite direction. Because the program requires animations for avatar bodies to move, users who choose animal avatars find themselves unable to use furniture at many social functions in Second Life. Book groups, for example, use chairs for their participants. Animal or inanimate object avatars have to stand on the outside of the group rather than sitting like other participants to avoid appearing deformed or irregular. Their interaction with other residents is, therefore, limited because the programming of the space privileges the use of human avatars, also demonstrating the interconnectedness of the limits of the program with the community structure of Second Life.

While Second Life, on the surface, appears to be a place where users can explore genderlessness as part of their identities, the boundaries of the space set irregular bodies apart from the other residents of the world.[33] Genderless, nonhuman bodies are defined in opposition to standard human bodies. While the virtual community might accept them openly, the program itself sets these bodies apart as Other. Because Second Life made standard human bodies the first avatars available to residents, habitus grew around that decision, privileging the human avatar. When a new resident enters Second Life, they encounter this boundary, which becomes a factor in how they create their identity. If they choose a hippo avatar, for example, their interactions with other users will change because of the ways in which the program privileges human avatar bodies over nonhuman or irregular bodies. Programmers may not be conscious of the types of performance limits they establish when they first begin creating virtual spaces. Yet their decisions have lasting impacts on the digital identities that result from such interactions, and how individuals can perform within a given space.

The creators of both Yik Yak and Second Life made specific decisions in creating these virtual spaces, and while programmers of such spaces may not have intended to limit performance, their choices control how users represent themselves within virtual spaces. Perhaps most importantly, such limitations dictate how individual users behave within virtual environments. Despite this, virtual spaces tend to be treated as neutral zones where users perform free of physical restrictions. Sherry Turkle has described virtual worlds as "laboratories" for identity creation, calling up the image of a sterile, neutral space for identity to grow.[34] However, this assertion ignores the extent to which online identity depends on the programmed reality within each virtual space. While some platforms require very little from the user when they sign up for a service, others require the new user to create an identity, complete with a new name and body. These new identities require a commitment from users to comply with the standards of each online community.[35] Since the programmed structure of each space influences virtual community standards, researchers and programmers should consider the ways in which even their indirect influence determines identity creation through community habitus.

Notes

1. John McCarthy and Peter Wright, "Technology as Experience," *interactions* 11, no. 5 (September/October 2004): 42–43.

2. Julian Dibbell, "A Rape in Cyberspace: Or How an Evil Clown, a Haitian Trickster Spirit, Two Wizards, and a Cast of Dozens Turned a Database into a Society," *New York Annual Survey of American Law* 471 (1994): 471.

3. John Perry, *Identity, Personal Identity, and the Self* (Indianapolis: Hackett Publishing, 2002).

4. Erving Goffman, *The Presentation of Self in Everyday Life* (Gloucester, Mass.: Peter Smith Publisher, 1999).

5. Joan Morris DiMicco and David R. Millen, "Identity Management: Multiple Presentations of Self in Facebook," *Proceedings of the 2007 International ACM Conference on Supporting Group Work* (New York: ACM, 2008), 383–86.

6. Dave Elder-Vass, "Reconciling Archer and Bourdieu in an Emergentist Theory of Action," *Sociological Theory* 25, no. 4 (December 2007): 325–46.

7. Margaret Archer, "Can Reflexivity and Habitus Work in Tandem?," in *Conversations about Reflexivity*, ed. Margaret S. Archer (New York: Routledge, 2009), 123–34.

8. Pierre Bourdieu, *Outline of a Theory of Practice* (New York: Cambridge University Press, 1977), 72.

9. Ibid.

10. "Yik Yak Homepage," Yik Yak, http://www.yikyakapp.com.

11. Yik Yak collects no user data when signing up. The user's phone number is the identifying marker that distinguishes each yak, but that information is not stored by the company. Location data and time of posting are saved by the company. While yaks are anonymous and cannot be traced by anyone using the app, police and other law enforcement agencies have used the information collected by the company to track down users who have posted yaks with threats to others. In September 2014, a student at the University of Georgia, Ariel Omar Arias, posted a yak from his phone while on campus. The yak read, "If you want to live don't be at the MLC [the Miller Learning Center] at 12:15." In less than an hour, using wifi locations, cell tower pings, and other location information, UGA police narrowed the search down to Arias and arrested him without incident. See Joe Johnson, "UGA Student Who Made Social Media Threat Suggesting Violence to Have Bond Hearing," *Athens Banner Herald*, September 23, 2014, http://onlineathens.com/local-news/2014-09-22/uga-student-who-made-social-media-threat-suggesting-violence-have-bond-hearing.

12. Justin Pot, "10 Things You Need to Know about Yik Yak," *Make Use Of* (blog), January 28, 2015, http://www.makeuseof.com/tag/10-things-need-know-yik-yak/.

13. Elyse Betters, "What Is Yik Yak? It's Like a Bathroom Stall Wall and Teens Are Cray Cray for It," *Pocket Lint* (blog), April 23, 2015, http://www.pocket-lint.com/news/133253-what-is-yik-yak-it-s-like-a-bathroom-stall-wall-and-teens-are-cray-cray-for-it.

14. Yaks captured at 2:04 pm, April 5, 2015, University of Georgia Yak feed.

15. Bending back again refers to the theory of reflexivity previously outlined in this article. For another particular reference to bending back, see Margaret Archer, *Making Our Way through the World: Human Reflexive and Social Mobility* (Cambridge: Cambridge University Press, 2007), 11.

16. Bourdieu, *Outline of a Theory.*

17. Hot List Yaks captured at 2:05 pm, April 5, 2015, University of Georgia Yak feed.

18. Robert Rotenberg and Gary McDonough, *The Cultural Meaning of Urban Space* (London: Bergin and Garvey, 1993).

19. This yak was posted with a recycle emoji, indicating that the original poster knew that the yak was recycled but believed it to be new enough to the community to warrant a posting. The fact that the yak was on the hot list shows that the poster guessed correctly.

20. Alyson Shontell, "How 2 Georgia Fraternity Brothers Created Yik Yak, a Controversial App that Became a ~$400 Million Business in 365 Days," *Business Insider*, March 12, 2015, http://www.businessinsider.com/the-inside-story-of-yik-yak-2015-3.

21. Tianna Smith's *Facebook* page, accessed March 28, 2015, https://www.facebook.com/photo.php?fbid=10205173882839028&set=pb.1003935496.-2207520000.1431538346.&type=3&theater.

22. Thomas Gieryn, "A Space for Place in Sociology," *Annual Review of Sociology* 26 (2000): 464–65.

23. Mesh refers to digital points stretched into a shape that is then animated based on those points and is used in all digital animation, including Second Life. Like a complicated web, these mesh bodies allow animators to program movement into what would commonly be static. A skin lies on top of the mesh to give the illusion of shadow, highlights, and features. See "Mesh," *Second Life Wiki*, http://wiki.secondlife.com/wiki/Mesh, accessed August 24, 2015.

24. Cory Ondrejka, "Escaping the Gilded Cage: User-Created Content and Building the Metaverse," in *The State of Play: Law, Games, and Virtual Worlds*, ed. Jack M. Balkin and Beth Simone Noveck (New York: New York University Press, 2006), 153.

25. A sim is a digital land area that can take various forms. When an avatar enters a sim area, the program translates the objects located into that area into graphics that are then viewable on the user's screen. Every sim starts as an empty, flat field 264 meters square. Machine-based coding creates the illusion of a natural world,

but in fact everything in a sim represents multiple users' manipulation of the program to create the illusion of objects. Regions, homesteads, and mainland are all types of sim with different maximum object counts. See "Regions," *Second Life Wiki*, August 3, 2014, http://wiki.secondlife.com/wiki/Region#Region; Tom Boellstorff, *Coming of Age in Second Life: An Anthropologist Explores the Virtually Human* (Princeton, N.J.: Princeton University Press, 2008), 12.

26. As a point of clarification, residents create objects to either keep for themselves or to sell. A variety of stores cater to all the whims of Second Life citizens, displaying goods that include clothing, transportation, homes, furniture, and many other objects designed to enhance a user's Second Life experience. While most residents do not make all of the items they use and enjoy inworld, the items are made by residents within the virtual society. See Boellstorff, *Coming of Age in Second Life*, 97–98.

27. Pierre Bourdieu, "Participant Objectivation," *Journal of the Royal Anthropological Institute* 9, no. 2 (June 2003): 281–94.

28. Mesh is the skeleton of points that allows a digital body to move (see note 23). The user manipulates these points through a shape, which gives the resident power over things such as shoulder width, leg length, and muscle thickness. The program regulates how much a user can manipulate the shape with thirty-seven different features that can be altered on a sliding scale of one to one hundred; each user must choose a male or female shape to begin with; and the body features then correspond to the biological markers associated with that gender. A male avatar's jaw, for example, can be more or less square, while a female avatar's jaw can be more or less rounded. Other sliders are more overtly named. For the first eight years of Second Life's existence, male avatars had a slider called "Package" that would increase the bulge in their crotch from "Coin Purse" to "Duffel Bag." A skin is the texture placed over the shape to give the illusion of skin. See Michael Rymaszewski et al., *Second Life: The Official Guide* (Indianapolis: Wiley, 2007), 82–86.

29. Kyra Grosman found that over seventy percent of both male and female users engaged in gender play during their second lives. In addition to simply switching genders, many residents opt for fantasy or alternative gender play within the world. See Kyra Grosman, "An Exploratory Study of Gender Swapping and Gender Identity in Second Life," PhD diss., Wright Institute, 2010.

30. Second Life avatar bodies mimic the signs of the biological body, but they represent a symbol of performance alone in the virtual world. Avatar bodies do not have organs, but the coding behind the image gives the illusion of a biological body. The gender when performed is composed of elements of biology (how the body is molded to fit a specific cultural expectation for gender based on coding), identity (the internal preference of the user), and expression (the outward behaviors and symbols). See Anne Fausto-Sterling, *Sex/Gender: Biology in a Social World* (New York: Routledge, 2012), 43–69.

31. Each new user chooses a starter avatar as their initial body when entering the virtual space. When Second Life first opened in 2003, starter avatars were easy to distinguish from other residents because of the poor quality of their skins, their

basic clothing made with basic textures (e.g., jeans and a T-shirt), and a single animation for walking. Older residents in this early world had clothes with better texture images to more closely approximate cloth, hand-drawn skins to give the illusion of flesh, and multiple animations to make their avatars move more naturally. Today, there are more than fifty starter avatars available to Second Life residents, and these avatars are of such high quality that they are almost indistinguishable from the rest of the Second Life population. The 2003 starter avatars were strictly human. Today, starter avatars can include nonhuman shapes and forms, but the mesh underneath those forms remains human. For examples of starter avatars, see Linden Lab, "New Mesh Avatars Available in Second Life," *Second Life* (blog), May 5, 2014, https://community.secondlife.com/t5/Featured-News/New-Mesh-Avatars-Now-Available-in-Second-Life/ba-p/2720912. The important point about starter avatars is that the avatar body is not a biological body but a constructed object. The program itself guides users to making a choice of a body that imitates biological bodies that are gendered. This choice also forces users into a specifically gendered performance because one aspect of gender, gender expression, or the sign, symbols, and presentation of gender through the body, is built in through the way the mesh is manipulated. The basic male mesh shape, for example, builds in a rugged, muscular presentation associated with body builders and hyper-masculine presentations of gender. While in the actual world, biology cannot be conflated with gender, the programming of Second Life makes it difficult to extract an alternatively gendered expression from the male and female meshes. In my discussion of genderless and/or gendered bodies in the virtual world, I in no way intend to collapse biological sex and gender as we understand it in the actual world. However, in the world of Second Life, the illusion of biological sex created by the programming behind the digital avatar body and gender are essentially collapsed because the gender biology of the digital body is programmed to read as gendered-male and gendered-female. In order to acknowledge the collapsing of sex and gender in Second Life, I refer to Second Life avatars as having "gendered" bodies. For a more nuanced view of the relationship of sex and gender, see Judith Butler, *Undoing Gender* (New York: Routledge, 2004), 184–86. For an explanation of gender expression, see Butler, *Gender Trouble: Feminism and the Subversion of Identity* (New York: Routledge, 1990), 18.

32. Male and female bodies operate differently within this virtual space. Each body has a specific mesh parameter that forces the bodies to appear more feminine or more masculine. Female mesh bodies, for example, cannot have shoulders as wide as male avatars' shoulders, and male avatars cannot have as large a pelvic area as female avatars. For a discussion of community standards on female and male body shapes as well as the shape underneath, see Vaelissa Cortes, "Creating a Well-Proportioned Shape," *SL Universe* (discussion board), January 17, 2011, http://www.sluniverse.com/php/vb/tutorials/54131-creating-well-proportioned-shape.html.

33. For a full discussion of genderless bodies in all of their forms in Second Life, see J. A. Brown, Meg Y. Brown, and Jennifer Regan, "Noobs, Moobs, and Boobs: An Exploration of Identity Formation in *Second Life*," in *Women and*

Second Life: Essays on Virtual Identity, Work, and Play (Jefferson, N.C.: McFarland, 2013), 45–62.

34. Sherry Turkle, *Life on the Screen: Identity in the Age of the Internet* (New York: Simon and Schuster, 2011), 12.

35. Meadows, 56–57. Mark Stephen Meadows, I, Avatar: The Culture and Consequences of Having a Second Life (New York: New Riders Press, 2007), 56–7.

Theatre Symposium 24

Closing Remarks

Sunday, April 12, 2015

Marvin Carlson

As far as summing up the conference, this is of course a formidable task, because so much ground has been covered. Let me remind you that historically we have gone from classic Greek, not just to the present productions that are running right now, like *Then She Fell* and Blue Man Group, but also things that go on into the future. We have heard about positive things like the Ottawa Arts Center, or, more negatively, surveillance, which is going to be even more part of our world in the future. We've hit the Renaissance, the nineteenth century, and so on. The historical range has been great; so, of course, has been the geographical range. We have had papers all the way from the West—California, to New York, and so on, to India, to the Chinese theatre, to the wonderful survey of cultural shows, to Southeast Asia and the theatre in Vietnam. It's been a real world tour. And obviously it's ranged very, very broadly in topics and approaches. Many of the major theorists and theoretical structures have been nicely illuminated during the discussions. We've had papers that had to do with a particular analysis of a particular text, and then going on out from the text into productions and production analysis, and on out from productions into places of theatre within the community—the social implications and political implications of theatre. That's my introduction.

[Laughter from the symposium participants]

As I say, it's a major task to put all this together. But let me go back through a person who's been quoted as recently as about an hour ago: Peter Brook's *Empty Space*. As many of you know, I have taken strong issue with it. But I want again to repeat the quotation from this morning that Peter Brook has famously said: "I can take an empty space and call it a stage." And people have often picked up and built upon, reasonably, that idea of the theatre being called into existence—what you might call the appellation of theatre. But the citation this morning also noted that Peter Brook goes on to say that in the process of taking that empty space and calling it a theatre, you need to bring somebody in to accept that and look at it. And that really takes us back through Peter Brook to an earlier period of theatrical theory—the early 1960s—when we were all in the grip, or coming into the grip, of high modernism. And one of the great questions for all the arts in high modernism was: What is the essence of this art? What is the essence of drama? What is the essence of music? What is the essence of —? And of course that then leads us in art to various kinds of minimalist art.

There were a number of statements in the sixties about [theatre]—strip everything else away, what is theatre? What is essential to theatre? And there were two quite famous statements about that, which overlap to a certain extent. Particularly, I want to talk about Eric Bentley's idea in *The Life of the Drama*, where he said, if you really want to take theatre down to its essence—and people have quoted this with a lot of different variations—what Bentley actually said was: "A imitates B while C watches." That's the essence of theatre. A person almost equally well known then, who has faded some, although Bentley has also faded as time has passed, is Richard Southern and his book *The Seven Ages of Theatre*, which came out in '61; Bentley was '64. Southern said, if we start taking things away— and the seven ages, each age another thing has been added to the theatre—costumes, scenery, and so on. When he gets back to the very beginnings of theatre, he says what we have is the performer and the observer. You split those apart, and theatre doesn't exist anymore.

Now, those two statements, of course, are rather similar. Neither one of them, notice, unlike Peter Brook, directly addresses space. Southern describes an action or a relationship—and indeed, to some extent, so does Bentley. It's a functional matter: A does something and imitates B, and C does something, watches. Now, looking back to these statements we realize they are both very heavily spatial. You really can't watch unless you're in a different space, but the space has to be contiguous to the first space or you can't watch. Now, I realize saying that, today with the media you can watch without being there, and that has implications also. But, as long as you're talking about the traditional, physical theatre, the assumption is that you have two spaces: one is the space of the watchers and one is the space of the watched. And we've come back to that again and again in different papers.

I'm going to focus, really, on the Bentley configuration because he gives us all three of these parts, and particularly from a spatial angle. That is to say, A imitates B while C watches. The first thing I have to say about this is that straightforward as this is, there are problems with it, especially in terms of contemporary performance. And the biggest problem today is major scholars have attacked mimesis—it's as simple as that. Probably Hans-Thies Lehmann's book *Postdramatic Theatre* is the most famous example of that, but there are a lot people around who have said, "No, no, you really don't have to have mimesis." And although I don't know that Lehmann has been cited in the conference, certainly many of the papers have had to do with, as it were, non-mimetic theatre: theatre that is created not because somebody imitates something, but because somebody is going to see, while C watches.

I think we can thank performance studies for that, which really began the erosion of mimesis by saying it isn't so much a matter of creating a character as performing an action, performing a meaningful action. And then you go back to Austin and people like that. So that what it is called in performance is "A consciously decides to do something to be observed and interpreted, which C watches." Mimesis has disappeared; you're really talking about the creation of a meaningful, or hoped-for meaningful action, which may be mimetic, but it may not be mimetic. I'll come back to this in a moment because there's another problematic about mimetics, but let me go back now again to each part of this.

A imitates B. Let's just think about A for a moment; A is whoever or whatever group, organization, structure decides to produce something which they call theatre, or theatrical activity. A number of the papers have quite reasonably focused on A, and A's control and one of the major questions in contemporary theatre is who's in control here? Who's doing it? Who's deciding what's to be done? And of course when we get into the immersive theatre, which has been addressed in several papers, this becomes a really critical question. A then becomes a kind of producing organization that sets up a kind of open-ended situation and C no longer merely watches, but C participates and, at least in theory, is a co-creator with A of the experience that happens. But traditionally, A has been pretty much in control of the game; C has been considered as a passive consumer of what A produces to be consumed, and many of the papers have dealt with that dynamic, that sort of concern. Whether it's the priming of the audience by Blue Man Group or the California theatre with its control of the audience, or even T. S. Eliot's *Murder in the Cathedral*, by and large the group in charge pretty well makes up the rules and decides what's going on. And so, we've had a number of papers that have talked about space from the aspect of A's creation of and control of a particular space.

If we go over the middle part of this: A imitates B—or, some people say, A pretends to be B—put aside for a moment the challenge to mimesis and just go directly to the process of mimesis. For most of theatre history mimesis has been a doubling, an assumption of another character, another persona that you are not. And you may say, well, this is a psychological or a relational operation, not a spatial one. Yes, the actor and the character inhabit the same space, but if you think of space, as a number of the papers have done, not as a physical but as a psychic matter, then of course what makes a character different from an actor is the psychic space between them. I am both this and I am that, but I put a psychic space between me and my creation. And a number of papers have talked about that psychic space, and indeed a couple of papers have gone perhaps a step further and talked about a particular kind of psychic space, and that is the psychic space of parody. That is to say, just as I can separate myself from a character, a play or a performance can separate itself from something else that the audience can see as psychically different from them. Whether it is the psychic difference in, let's say, Ira Aldridge and Matthews, the psychic difference of the black and white interpretation. Or whether it is, to take a more common example, the psychic difference that is involved when you're doing Opera on Tap or country music that is both real country music and a kind of parody or takeoff of country music. Whether you're doing real opera or a kind of parody or takeoff. Now, that is not to say, and neither of these papers tried to say, that the parody cheapens the work; on the contrary, it provides a richer perspective of the work, a different kind of space. And it does go back again to mimesis because with parody, since you are making a conscious spatial distance between the already known original and the takeoff on the original, you are calling the audience's attention to the fact that you as a performer are not being mimetic, but you're standing outside and commenting on something, or, if you like, you're being mimetic of something else. When you're doing Opera on Tap it may be that you're singing a Mozart aria, but you are also "singing" a Mozart aria—that is, you are both conscious of the character and the fact that a performer is doing it. That's sort of built into parody because of what you're doing. And the same thing of course is also true of the country music show. They are at one and the same time doing the real thing, and also, as it were, winking at you and saying, "We're performers, notice what we're doing with this." That's what parody always involves— that kind of spatial distance between—not only between the original material and what you're seeing, but also between the original performance style and assumptions about what a character is and the performer who is in fact doing it. It's for that reason that it has often been remarked that parody goes much beyond simple making fun of something; it is making fun of and celebrating something at the same time. There's always a kind of doubleness in that, so that the question of mimesis and the space in mimesis has come in [to the symposium] in a number of different ways.

I mentioned earlier the decline or the questioning of mimesis in contemporary culture. When you try to get rid of mimesis, then what if anything do you put in its place? And I would point, again, to the model that we see in performance studies, or the anti-mimetic side of performance studies where you're sort of talking about the Austinian performative: something that is consciously produced in order to have a particular kind of effect or produce another kind of action to create a performance. Then, it shifts away from performance toward observation. The difference between—if there is a difference—between brushing your teeth in front of your bathroom mirror and my pulling out a toothbrush now and brushing my teeth—is that you're there watching. That's what makes it into a performance, in the simplest sense. Performance is something done for somebody. It's not just done. Now, you may say, "Ah, but am I not my own performer in the bathroom mirror?" [Laughter.] That's another question; it's a different aspect of the problem, which I might as well go into right now [more laughter], which is the last part of this: "Who is the C anyway?" And what are they doing? And what is their responsibility?

Of course, in many of the papers the emphasis has been on C: the people who used to just watch but now in immersive theatre are drawn in and do other kinds of things. And we've looked at C in many different ways—in the way that C is controlled by spaces, or sought to be controlled, like the upstairs and downstairs racial entrances in the nineteenth-century American theatre, or the segregation of people in the California theatre, or indeed any of the theatres about which we have talked that explore how space is used within the theatre. Looking back over the history of theatre, it is of course a spatial art at the very beginning, not only because actors move through space, which actually not many of the papers have talked about—what we might call blocking, which is a very critical part of what we do in the theatre. But much more, the conference has focused, quite properly, in reflecting upon the concern that we have about theatre now, and that is the theatre as embedded in culture and in a society. Fifty years ago when you studied theatre, by and large you read plays and read about the theatres they were performed in and that was it. You didn't really think about what are the economics, what are the social, what are the ethnic implications, what are the class implications of this. Now we have a much more, I would say, sophisticated—I hate to be an evolutionist about this—but let's at least say a much broader interest in how theatre is operating not as a particular art form but as a product of human culture. And that not only allows us to ask, I think, richer and more interesting and more provocative questions, but also allows us to ask more global questions about theatre. We're not restricted to a particular model. It also—and I think this is critical—challenges us to ask more social and political questions about theatre. What is it doing? Who's in control? Who's profiting? And so on. And all those come out of that kind of consideration. So obviously, C and the relationship between C and A now takes on a different kind of relationship and it, in part, involves power. Who is in control? What kind of control does A exercise over C—or should they exercise over C? The particular sort of space traditionally that C occupies has been a space established and controlled by A—and that still is essentially true. I noticed even in the Algonquin Group there was a rope around A so that C was excluded.

Now, that rope around the Algonquin Group actually raises a number of interesting questions. The most obvious thing, of course, as with most traditional theatre, is not only who's in but also who's out. Who is allowed to—and this is where [Jacques] Rancière comes in—is there any emancipation given to C or is C totally outside the rope and not in any way involved with this? But also, the various spatial configurations we've talked about and I mentioned already—the Cs that are outside the rope—how are they differentiated? Or indeed, even who is allowed to be outside the rope? Not everybody can go to the Algonquin. And here we get into this very important question about access to theatre. We discussed the term "invisibility." How you can pass into a theatre without being challenged, which has of course not only the obvious racial implications, but also class implications, and that's always been an important part of theatre. Sometimes [it has been] legislated very specifically and other times just if you're a certain kind of person you don't go to the Bowery Theatre. If you're a certain kind of person you don't go to the African Grove Theatre or the Park Theatre, or whatever. So, there's always been some of that sort of thing.

But to go back to the Algonquin—there is a rope around these people. And when I call your attention to that it means I am making a model in which [Alexander] Woollcott and Dorothy Parker and that gang are performers. Did they think of themselves as performers? I would say yes. And what does mimesis have to do with this? Is Alexander Woollcott playing Alexander Woollcott? I would say, absolutely. No question. No question. All of these people were performing. Dorothy Parker? Obviously. Bentley—I mean, part of what they did was that they performed for each other. And I doubt, frankly, if any one of them would have denied it, because these are very sophisticated people and very self-aware people. Certainly Oscar Wilde, whom they all loved, was well aware that he was playing a part. He did that very consciously and reveled in it, and I can't believe that Dorothy Parker was not equally conscious. But then this raises another question, that is—how porous is the question of mimesis? In a certain sense is any consciously produced behavior mimetic? Am I not playing Marvin Carlson right now? Of course I am. [Laughter.] Of course I am. I'm in full costume. [More laughter.] The beard and everything. And very calculatedly doing this. And everybody, I think, in theatre is to some extent aware of this. And if we weren't we certainly were when Performance Studies came along and we started reading Erving Goffman and his like and said, "Look, it's all performative; it's all framing, it's all staging." The props [gestures to his water bottle], everything is here.

So that then introduces space, which is related to the space between actor and character. But [it] has to be looked at in a somewhat different way, and that is the space between whoever the real person is and the person who is being consciously performed. And of course if we go out into Judith Butler-land we may be talking about performance that is not even conscious but is still performing, is still the creation of a particular kind of character. So, a number of the papers have talked about those kinds of spaces. The spaces that C creates or C is involved in.

Having gone through A imitates B while C watches, let me go back and put them together again. What we're really talking about ultimately then is the most important space—the space that allows this to happen, encourages this to happen, or is found to make this happen. Very often in theatre history, of course, the space has been created or found or devised particularly with this in mind, from the Greek theatre onward. Although theatre has always both had to find spaces as the Bengali theatre does today, or maybe very consciously went to find spaces like *Murder in the Cathedral*, and utilized them in that way.

One item of space that hasn't been a great deal talked about, although several people, as for example with the Ottawa National Theatre, have talked about this, is the urban space. Where is a theatre located within the city and what does that mean? But it's always there. That is, you'll notice with the Bengali theatre one of the first things said is there's the North, the Central, and the South. Any theatre city has its areas and its locations. If it's in Decatur it's different than being in Atlanta. If it's uptown in New York it's very different from being downtown, and so on. If it's in the black neighborhood or in Harlem in New York it's obviously very different from being in the Upper East Side, or wherever it happens to be. So that's always been a consideration and a number of the papers touched on that. More touched upon internal arrangements, but even more touched on something that's kind of in between these, which is, I think, very important and, again, very indicative of our modern idea of theatre.

We used to think theatre was a space. Now we much more think theatre is a concept; it's a way that a certain space is used, as Peter Brook suggests. But I'm particularly thinking that within theatre history, the theatres that have had the closest connection to their society and the most support from their society have been theatres with a really solid permanent space like the Comédie Française or the Theatre Dionysus. However, in the nineteenth century, especially toward the end of the nineteenth century, many people began to say, "Yes, but those theatres are monuments to high culture and a particular social class. What about the people out there who never go to those theatres, that find that space wrong or intimidating?" There are several answers to that—the most obvious is, of course, go out where they are. And so you get ambulatory theatres. You get El Teatro Campesino, which has been mentioned. Firmin Gémier with his rolling theatre in the 1890s; Joe Papp with his mobile theatre, which still runs regularly out to disadvantaged New York neighborhoods and takes theatre to the people. All these are based upon, not only an idea of space, but also of taking the space around to other places. In a way, I wouldn't even say colonizing, which is an unfortunate word, but opening up spaces for theatre elsewhere. Converting spaces into a different kind of consciousness and a different kind of use. And I think that's another way that theatre spaces are imported around. I do not advise or support the Bengali solution—which is not a solution, but a necessity—of running around and performing in a variety of different spaces. That's very difficult, and I offer my greatest praise to people who work under those conditions. On the other hand, there is something very positive about theatre that goes all over everywhere and plays in a lot of different neighborhoods and many modern theatres, as some of the papers have mentioned, have taken advantage of that.

The theatre is perhaps today, even though it's a challenged art, an art that can be found in a greater variety of spaces all around the world than at any time in the past. Partly it's an economic matter. But partly it is a conscious choice of taking theatre into communities, into social classes, into all kinds of areas that have not had it or known it or been aware of how that sort of space can be created or what it might mean. Now that's the positive side. Here's the negative side—and here I go to James Fisher's paper on surveillance. If we now say that theatre and theatrical space are as much created by C as by A, then we get into the very interesting question of "What happens when C takes charge?" What happens when the observer takes charge? And I think James illustrated this very clearly by taking the same event, a street performance, not necessarily by Brecht, but indeed by any kind of political street performance. Just go back to the sixties and throw a rock. There were plenty of people doing this. The idea, of course, behind those performances (whether mimesis was involved or not, and it usually was) was, of course, that the A that was imitating B was doing this for the C that was gathered around them in the public park or whatever, to be energized, influenced, inspired by that activity. Now that can still happen and does still happen, but as James says, at the same time up in a tree nearby is an observance camera. There is another C. And who is that C, and what do they do, and how does it affect these operations? It's an updating of the panopticon concern. And really gives rise not only to political concerns, but also to theoretical concerns. Certainly in demonstrations today, you are demonstrating largely not for the people around you but for the cameras. You know you're being observed. That's part of the game. So when A is imitating B for C, the C can be a variety of things for a variety of reasons now.

So when we talk about space what does space mean here? Already when we moved into digital performance these questions became much more complicated. If you're in Second Life as we [considered] in some of the discussion, then what you are is you are A creating a C which pretends to be B. Or I'll put it another way—you're everything. But you're not everything. You're controlling a character who is also sort of your actor, but that's also yourself. You're watching yourself doing these things—as actors of course always have done, in a sense. They're always their own C as well. But as also was pointed out in the paper, we're still not talking Rancière here. That is, you're still playing by the rules that are set up by that particular game. But already in the digital world, space becomes much more flexible and much more negotiable than it was before, and of course the surveillance world just extends that out further. We now can truly say that an action that is performed by A—the C is infinite. The C can be anywhere and anybody. And in a way that also makes the A and the imitation of B also able, potentially, to take any space, because it can be watched and reproduced everywhere. The theatre has become then truly—or performance, mimetic or not—has become truly a global operation. This is potentially a very Orwellian, depressing idea. But it's also, it seems to me, potentially a utopian idea. It really depends on how the spatial negotiations and the power relationships that are always embedded in spatial relationships are going to be negotiated in the future.

Contributors

Arnab Banerji is an assistant professor of theatre history, literature, and dramaturgy at Loyola Marymount University, Los Angeles, where he teaches courses on theatre history, Asian theatre, and dramaturgy. His primary area of research interest is contemporary Indian performance. Arnab was one of the ASIANetwork Luce Foundation Postdoctoral Teaching Fellows during the 2014–2015 academic year at Muhlenberg College and also taught at Barnard College, Columbia University during Spring 2015. Arnab is the recipient of the 2015 David Keller Travel Award from ASTR. His essays on Indian performance and reviews of contemporary scholarship on Asian performance have appeared in the *Asian Theatre Journal*, *Theatre Journal*, and *Southeastern Review of Asian Studies*.

Becky K. Becker, *Theatre Symposium* editor, is assistant director for the Center for International Education and professor of theatre at Columbus State University. In addition to her involvement with the Southeastern Theatre Conference, she is vice chair of the National Playwriting Program for Region IV of the Kennedy Center American College Theatre Festival. Her research includes cross-cultural theatre, intercultural communication, new plays, and embodied cognition. Her work has appeared in *Theatre Journal, Feminist Teacher, Review: The Journal of Dramaturgy, Theatre Symposium*, and various edited volumes.

Lisa Marie Bowler is a London-based dramaturg currently completing her doctoral thesis on theatre architecture and embodiment at the Ludwig-Maximilians-Universität in Munich, Germany. A classically trained former dancer, she is particularly interested in the relationship between the moving body and its surrounding space. She worked at Sadler's Wells Theatre in London for several years and specializes in dance dramaturgy. She has also worked at Shakespeare's Globe and in 2014 participated in the Mellon School of Theatre & Performance Research at Harvard University.

Chase Bringardner is an associate professor of theatre at Auburn University who specializes in the study of popular entertainments such as medicine shows and musical theatre, regional identity construction, and intersections of gender, race, and class in popular performance forms. He works regularly as a director, recently staging Caryl Churchill's *Vinegar Tom* in the fall of 2014. He has written a chapter in *The Oxford Companion to the Musical* on region, politics, and identity in musical theatre as well as publications in other journals, including *Theatre Journal* and *Theatre Topics*. His current book-length project posits a framework for a regional analysis of musical theatre history, focusing explicitly on a genealogy of the "southern" musical. He is an active member of the Association for Theatre in Higher Education, where he currently serves as vice president of membership and marketing.

Marvin Carlson is the Sidney E. Cohn Professor of Theatre, Comparative Literature, and Middle Eastern Studies at the Graduate Center of the City University of New York. He has received an honorary doctorate from the University of Athens, the ATHE Career Achievement Award, the ASTR Distinguished Scholarship Award, the George Jean Nathan Award for Dramatic Criticism, the Rosenblum Award for Contributions to Theatre and Education, and the Calloway Prize for writing in theatre. He is the founding editor of the journal *Western European Stages*. He is the author of twenty-one books, the most recent of which, written with Khalid Amine, is *The Theatres of Morocco, Algeria and Tunisia* (Palgrave, 2012).

Alicia Corts is an assistant professor of theatre at Saint Leo University. She is also a founding member of WITS, the Women in Theatre in the Southeast project. She has directed off-Broadway and across the United States. She received her PhD in theatre from the University of Georgia, and her research deals with virtual performance. She has published in *Ecumenica* and *Theatre Journal* as well as contributed chapters to *The Immersive Internet: Reflections on the Entangling of the Virtual with Society, Politics, and the Economy, The Retro-Futurism of Cute*, and *Open Systems/Closed Worlds*.

Andrew Gibb is assistant professor and head of history, theory, and criticism in the Department of Theatre and Dance at Texas Tech University. He writes about Chicana/o theatre and performance in the nineteenth-century US West. His work has appeared in *Theatre History Studies*, the *Journal of Dramatic Theory and Criticism*, the *Latin American Theatre Review, Comparative Drama*, and in the collection *Querying Difference in Theatre History* (Cambridge Scholars, 2007).

Sarah McCarroll, associate editor of *Theatre Symposium*, is an assistant professor of theatre at Georgia Southern University, where she teaches courses such as theatre history, costume design, and script analysis. She holds a PhD in theatre history, theory, and literature from Indiana University and an MFA in Costume Design from the University of Alabama. Her article "The 'Boy' Who Wouldn't Grow Up: Peter Pan and the Dangers of Eternal Youth" appeared in *Theatre Symposium* 23. Since 2003, her professional home has been the Utah Shakespeare Festival, where she has worked as a dramaturg, first hand, and wardrobe supervisor. Sarah is the current chair of SETC's History/Theory/Criticism/Literature committee.

Samuel T. Shanks is an instructor in the theatre program at the University of Minnesota, Duluth. His interests range from early American theatre to Islamic theatre, and from acting theory to cognitive studies.

Sebastian Trainor is a visiting assistant professor of theatre at Saint Lawrence University in northern New York. He is currently researching "secret" histories of famous theatrical events, an ongoing project intended to help revise misleading accounts associated with some of our canonical theatre narratives. His essays have appeared in *Text & Presentation, Journal of American Drama and Theatre*, and, most recently, in the collection *Women in the Arts in the Belle Epoque: Essays on Influential Artists, Writers and Performers* (McFarland, 2014).

Christine Woodworth is an assistant professor of theatre at Hobart & William Smith Colleges, where she teaches courses in theatre history and literature and regularly directs. Woodworth is coeditor (with Elizabeth Osborne) of *Working in the Wings: New Perspectives on Theatre History and Labor*. Her work has appeared in *Theatre Symposium, Theatre History Studies, Theatre Annual, Text and Presentation*, and a number of edited collections. She is a member of the Lincoln Center Directors Lab and a past participant in the LaMaMa Umbria International Symposium for Directors, Directors Lab North, SITI Summer Theater Workshop, the Mellon School of Theater and Performance Research at Harvard University, and the NEH Summer Institute on Roman Comedy in Performance.